Mission in the Old Testament

Other Books by Walter C. Kaiser, Jr.

Mission in the Old Testament

Israel as a Light to the Nations

WALTER C. KAISER, JR.

BakerBooks

A Division of Baker Book House Co
Grand Rapids, Michigan 49516

© 2000 by Walter C. Kaiser, Jr.

Published by Baker Books
a division of Baker Book House Company
P.O. Box 6287, Grand Rapids, MI 49516-6287

Third printing, November 2002

Printed in the United States of America

Library of Congress Cataloging-in-Publication Data

Kaiser, Walter C.
    Mission in the Old Testament : Israel as a light to the nations / Walter C. Kaiser, Jr.
        p.   cm.
    Includes bibliographical references (p.) and indexes.
    ISBN 0-8010-2228-2 (pbk.)
    1. Missions—Biblical teaching. 2. Bible. O.T.—Criticism, interpretation, etc.
    I. Title.
    BS1199.M53 K35   2000
    266'.009'01—dc21   99-050219

For information about academic books, resources for Christian leaders, and all new releases available from Baker Book House, visit our web site:
                    http://www.bakerbooks.com

Contents

To the faithful teachers of missions and evangelism,
all former or present colleagues and faithful friends:

In memory of:
Mrs. Fran Hiebert
Dr. Herb and Winnie Kane
Dr. J. Christy Wilson, Jr.

And with appreciation for:
Dr. Robert and Mariette Coleman
Dr. David and Gertrude Hesselgrave
Dr. Paul Hiebert
Dr. Art and Muriel Johnston
Dr. Peter and Vlasta Kuzmič
Dr. Lois McKinney
Dr. John and Peggy Nyquist
Dr. Ed and Annie Rommen
Dr. Tim and Julie Tennet
Dr. Tim and Eleanor Warner
Mrs. Betty Wilson

Preface

PROBABLY THE last thing a person is likely to think about in connection with the Old Testament is a missionary message to the Gentiles and the nations of the world. That begins, we are assured by less careful readers of the Old Testament, in the New Testament after our Lord gave the Great Commission (Matt. 28:18–20; Mark 16:15) and the promised Holy Spirit had come on the disciples (Acts 1:8). Of course this New Testament "Great Commission" was not simply a one-time statement in these two Gospels, but it was a repeated emphasis in the life and ministry of our Lord and in the Gospels (Luke 24:44–49; John 20:21).

But is this correct?

It is not! The Bible actually begins with the theme of missions in the Book of Genesis and maintains that driving passion throughout the entire Old Testament and on into the New Testament. If an Old Testament "Great Commission" must be identified, then it will be Genesis 12:3—"all the peoples of the earth will be blessed through you [Abraham]." This is the earliest statement of the fact that it will be God's purpose and plan to see that the message of his grace and blessing comes to every person on planet earth. The message did not begin there. The basis for it, in fact, went all the way back to Genesis 3:15, as will be seen shortly, but in Genesis 12:3 it found its most succinct declaration.

Likewise, the last book of Scripture emphasizes the same concern for people: "every nation and tribe and tongue and people" (Rev. 5:9; 7:9; 14:6). Thus this theme of a mission to the whole world forms one giant envelope (a figure of speech called an inclusio) framing the whole Bible, from Genesis to Revelation.

But some will object: Was it not God's plan in the Old Testament to give his message of salvation exclusively to the Jewish people first? Wasn't it only after several millennia that God eventually broadened his plan to embrace the Gentiles after the apostle Paul became frustrated in his attempts to reach his own Jewish people?

True enough, Paul did come to a dramatic conclusion in Acts 13:46–47 at the synagogue in Antioch Pisidia: "then Paul and Barnabas answered them boldly: 'We had to speak the word of God to you first. Since you reject it and do not consider yourselves worthy of eternal life, we now turn to the Gentiles. For this is what the Lord has commanded us:

> I have made you a light for the Gentiles,
> that you may bring salvation to the ends of the earth.'"

Before that, at the time of Paul's conversion on the road to Damascus, already the Lord had told Ananias, "Go, this is my chosen instrument to carry my name before the Gentiles and their kings and before the people of Israel" (Acts 9:15). Paul later confirmed this commission to go to the Gentiles at the time of his conversion when he gave his famous "Speech on the stairs" (Acts 22:15), and he repeated it to Agrippa (Acts 26:15–17). Way back then, God had said, "Go, I will send you far away to the Gentiles," which Paul describes as a foundational strategy (Acts 26:18). Therefore, it can hardly be argued that this was some sort of late shift in the apostolic plans and that it marked the first time that the message of salvation would now be extended to the non-Jewish world. In fact, Paul cites as his authority the Old Testament word from Isaiah 49:6—"It is too small a thing for you to be my servant. . . . I have also made you a light for the Gentiles, that you may bring my salvation to the ends of the earth."

Even Peter, who seems to be slower on the uptake of this idea, preaches about it in Acts 3:25–26. He even makes it the introduction to the Gentile household of Cornelius in Acts 10:34–35.

It would also be incorrect to say that Abraham was the first to receive the "all peoples" target for the message of the gospel. Genesis 1–11 was far from being a nationalistic section that favored the Jews. It is one of the most universalistic sections of the Bible, ending with a list in Genesis 10 of seventy nations—the very "families" and "all peoples" that were to receive the blessing from God through Abraham and his collective seed in Genesis 12:3.

The expression "all peoples" did not mean that every person on earth would universally believe in the Messiah, but that every ethnic group would receive this blessing of God's grace and the joy of participating in worshiping and serving him. God would do this both by his own sovereignty (for he bound himself by a unilateral oath, as we shall see later) and through the instrumentality of those who had previously experienced the blessing of God.

The blessing that would come through Abraham referred back to a blessing already announced after the fall of Adam and Eve. As God's antidote to the curse brought on by sin, a male descendant from the woman Eve was promised (Gen. 3:15). The curse affected the human race universally, but no less extensive in its healing potential was the promised antidote offered by God. This offer was enlarged, as we shall see, in the promise given to Shem (Gen. 9:27) and then to Abraham (Gen. 12:1–3).

But God's call to service and his election as instruments of his grace brought with it the obligation and responsibility to be a blessing to all the families of the earth. Exodus 19:4–6 describes Abraham's seed as a "moveable treasure," "a kingdom of priests," and "a holy nation" to carry out God's purposes. Especially significant is the description of Israel as a priesthood of believers. The priesthood was to serve God and to minister to others.

It is at this point that the thesis of this book participates in issues that are hotly debated today: Did this "kingdom of priests" serve Israel alone, or the entire world? Were they to be active or merely passive witnesses? Was Israel's role as mission with regard to the world *centripetal* (inward-moving, and therefore the people of that time were said to play a passive role in witnessing and spreading the Good News) or *centrifugal* (outward-moving, and therefore the Old Testament believers were active in sharing their faith)?[1]

Centrifugal witnessing, it will be argued here, is the role assigned to Israel in actively sharing with others the Man of Promise who was to come. This is why Paul quoted Isaiah 49:6 in his attempt to convince the Jews at Antioch of Pisidia that it had been God's intent all along to extend his blessings of redemption to the Gentiles (apart from any process of proselytism by which Gentiles converted to Judaism). And this will be our contention in this work as well. The source of world missionary activity is rooted in God's call to the nation Israel in the Old Testament.

Indeed, the apostle Paul himself maintained that his own call to be an apostle to the Gentiles easily paralleled similar calls of Jeremiah and Isaiah in the Old Testament (cf. Gal. 1:15–16; Isa. 49:1; and Jer. 1:5). He began his letter to the Romans with the affirmation that he was "called to

---

1. See Walter Vogels, "Covenant and Universalism: Guide for a Missionary Reading of the Old Testament," *Zeitschrift für Missionswissenschaft und Religionswissenschaft* 57 (1973): 31.

be an apostle," "set apart for the gospel of God which [God] promised beforehand through his prophets in the holy scriptures" (Rom. 1:1–2). His mission was to call Gentiles from "among the nations" (Rom. 1:5) to believe in Jesus Christ until the "full number of the Gentiles" (Greek: *plērōma tōn ethnōn* in Rom. 11:25) had been gathered in to Christ. Roger D. Aus suggested[2] that the "offering of the Gentiles" in Romans 15:16 would fulfill what the prophet Isaiah saw (Isa. 66:19–23). As a result of missionary activity, "all flesh" (Isa. 66:23), including Jews and Gentiles, would worship the Lord. They would come from as far away as Tarshish, that is, Spain[3] (Isa. 66:19), a site often linked with "from the end of the earth" (Ps. 72:8–11; Jonah 1:3).

The fact remains that the goal of the Old Testament was to see both Jews and Gentiles come to a saving knowledge of the Messiah who was to come. Anything less than this goal was a misunderstanding and an attenuation of the plan of God. God's eternal plan was to provide salvation for all peoples; it was never intended to be reserved for one special group, such as the Jews, even as an initial offer! It is the history of this offer and the way it was carried out in Old Testament times that will form the heart of our study here.

I must append an important note of appreciation. I am deeply indebted to my two missiology colleagues, Dr. Timothy Tennent and Dr. Peter Kuzmich, for their kindness in reading this manuscript. Several others performed the same sacrificial service and made a host of wonderful suggestions: Dr. Kenneth B. Mullholland of Columbia International University (while he was on sabbatical leave, no less), Dr. Paul G. Hiebert of Trinity Evangelical Divinity School, Greg H. Parsons, Executive Director of U. S. Center for World Missions, and Ralph Winter of the U. S. Center for World Missions in Pasadena, California. Their help was immensely appreciated. Naturally, any blemishes that still exist are my own despite their best efforts.

---

2. Roger D. Aus, "Paul's Travel Plans to Spain and the 'Full Number of the Gentiles' of Rom. XI 25," *Novum Testamentum* 21 (1979): 232–62. See especially pp. 234–35.

3. Tarshish or Tartessus was a Phoenician mercantile city in Spain. James Muilenberg, "The Book of Isaiah, Chapters 40–66," in *The Interpreter's Bible* (New York: Abingdon, 1956), 5:771.

Introduction

UP UNTIL the 1950s the subject of the missionary movement was referred to as "missions" in the plural form. In fact, the term "missions" was first used in its current context by the Jesuits in the sixteenth century. But the International Missionary Council discussions in the 1950s on the *missio Dei* convinced most that the mission of the Triune God was prior to any of the number of missions by Christians during the two millennia of church history. Consequently, since there was only one mission, the plural form has dropped out of familiar usage and the singular form, "mission," has replaced it for the most part. Nevertheless, most churches and lay-persons hang on to the plural missions. For that reason, and to make our point clear here, we will refer to it in this work from time to time while alerting believers to the coming change.

Around 1960 another term began to appear in English, even though it had been used frequently in Europe earlier: "missiology." This was the term used to designate the formal study of the Christian mission in its biblical, theological, historical, cultural, and strategic dimensions as well as its present and future aspects. While the word is not at home in English, since it has a partial Latin base *(missio)* with a Greek suffix *(logos)*, it appears to have gained wide enough acceptance to mark the discipline of mission from this point forward.

Mission points to a central action: the act of being *sent* with a commission to carry out the will of a superior. It is God who commissions and God who sends. And it is this word of "sending" that lexically links the Old Testament with the New Testament. The Hebrew word "to send," *šālaḥ*, is found over eight hundred times. Over two hundred times God is the subject of this verb in the Old Testament. The Greek New Testament word "to send" is *apostellō*. Interestingly enough, it is this Greek verb (or 11 a compound of it) that is used to translate three-fourths of passages in the Greek Septuagint where God is the subject of this verb.[1]

The most important feature of the divine sending of anyone on a mission is the will of the One who sent the emissary. While the Lord sends a variety of agents to accomplish all sorts of purposes, the most frequent association with God's sending is the office of prophet. Moses and his brother Aaron top this list. Repeatedly Moses is described as sent by the Lord (Exod. 3:10–15; Deut. 34:11; 1 Sam. 12:8; Ps. 105:26). Just as God sends his word (Isa. 55:11) and it accomplishes that for which it was sent, so God sent a whole line of prophets who would accomplish what God had intended (Isa. 6:8; Jer. 1:7; Ezek. 3:5–6). In fact, what distinguished the true prophet from the false, probably more than anything else, was the fact that God had not sent the false prophets (Jer. 14:14, 15; 23:21; 28:15; Ezek. 13:6). Over and over again, God sent his prophets throughout the history of Israel (2 Kings 17:13; Jer. 7:25; 25:4; 26:5; 29:19; Zech. 7:12).

It is not as if none of the Gentile nations are addressed in the Old Testament writings, for whole books are devoted to their involvement in the plan of God for worldwide redemption. For example, the book about the Moabite woman Ruth is central to the whole plan of God to send his Messiah through that very line. Likewise, the whole prophecy of Obadiah was addressed to the nation of Edom.

Also, large segments of the prophetic books are addressed to the nations abroad. Thus, the eighth-century prophet Isaiah, between his discussions of the first advent of Messiah in chapters 7–12 and the second advent of Messiah in chapters 24–27, addressed chapters 13–23 to ten foreign nations. The seventh-century prophet Jeremiah had a similar long section to the nations in chapters 46–52. Ezekiel, in the sixth century, discussed God's plan for the Gentile nations in chapters 25–32 while Jerusalem was under siege by the Babylonians. In a similar manner, the prophet Amos had begun his eighth-century prophecy in chapters 1 and 2 with his message to the nations.

To be sure, most of the words to these nations were messages of impending judgment, but so was the message of Jonah that brought deliverance and salvation to that nation. These same threats of divine judgment were wakeup calls from the prophets to turn to the Sovereign God of all the nations.

---

1. See Ferris L. McDaniel, "Mission in the Old Testament," in *Mission in the New Testament: An Evangelical Approach*, ed. William J. Larkin, Jr., and Joel F. Williams (Maryknoll, N.Y.: Orbis , 1998), pp. 12–13. See also Bernard Wodecki, "ŠHLH. dans le livre d'Isaie," *Vetus Testamentum* 34 (1984): 482–88.

Finally, Yahweh must send his people into exile in order for them to act in accordance with his desire that the nation of Israel should be his agents whereby he could bless all the families of the earth. First, there was the Assyrian exile of the ten northern tribes of Israel in 721 B.C. and then the Babylonian exile of Judah in 586 B.C. By means of these diaspora, or scatterings, the word of God would eventually be disseminated over large parts of the world of that day.

There would be individuals who would also be sent by a divine call to minister to others than their own people Israel. We will consider Melchizedek, Jethro, Balaam, Ruth, a captured Israelite maiden, and the reluctant prophet Jonah. All of them pointed, in their own way, to the grace of God.

It is our hope that the formative theology of Genesis 12:3 may once again be seen for what it is and has always been in the discussion of mission: a divine program to glorify himself by bringing salvation to all on planet earth. Indeed, here is where missions really begins. Here is the first Great Commission mandate of the Bible. It is this thesis that dominates the strategy, theology, and mission of the Old Testament. And it is this thesis that we unfold in this volume.

ONE

God's
Plan for Missions
in the Old Testament

NO ONE can charge the Old Testament with beginning its story in a chauvinistic way. Genesis 1–11 is decidedly universal in its scope and outlook. It covers as much time, even on a minimalist chronology of the events from the creation of the world in Genesis 1 until the call of Abraham in Genesis 12, as is found in the rest of the Old Testament. Rather than being pro-Jewish or featuring Israel as God's favored or pet nation (a view that is incorrectly applied to all of the Old Testament), Genesis 1–11 begins with the original human couple, Adam and Eve, and moves on until seventy nations[1] of the world are encompassed in the scope of its message (in the Table of Nations in Genesis 10).

The earth is filled with a multitude of peoples and nations by the time we finish the first eleven chapters of Genesis. All of this is a result of the blessing of God. In fact, "blessing," or the verb "to bless," is one of the key concepts of these chapters. It is this noun and verb that connects this

1. The word "nations" refers here, not so much, to the geo-political entities as it does to large groups of peoples usually in ethnic associations.

section of the book with the announcement of the promise-plan of God in Genesis 12:1–3, where the word "to bless" or "blessing" occurs five times.

But just as the blessing of God is at work from the creation of the world on, in like manner the earth was simultaneously being overwhelmed by one catastrophe after another. There were three such crises that fell on humanity as a result of their sin: (1) the fall, (2) the flood, and (3) the failure of the Tower of Babel. However, with each crisis came a promise from God that formed the worldwide blessing of God to all mortals.

The Three Crises and the Promise-Plan of God: Genesis 1–11

The scope and import of the word of God could not be more extensive than that given in the opening chapters of Genesis. The original couple, progenitors of the whole human race, failed the test of obedience that God had designed for them. Because they yielded to the temptation of the tempter in the Garden of Eden, a curse fell not only on Adam and Eve, but also on the ground, its products, the created order, and all humanity.

But the story did not end there, for in Genesis 3:15 God declared that he would put "enmity" between the Serpent and the woman, between the Serpent's "seed" and the woman's "seed." But then a sudden turn of events announced that the Serpent would bruise the heel of one of the woman's "seed," a male from among her offspring. Most surprising of all, however, the male child of the woman's "seed" would strike back by crushing the head of the Serpent. This would be a lethal blow. It guaranteed that the coming Man of Promise, from the male line of Eve, would once and for all settle the issues that the sin of Adam and Eve had raised.

How much of this prediction did Eve understand, much less those who read this story during Old Testament times? A strong hint is given to us in Genesis 4. When Eve conceived a son, she named him "Cain," saying, "I have brought forth a man, *even the* LORD" (Gen. 4:1). Most English versions translate this phrase something like "with the help of the LORD." However, the text simply has the direct object sign in the Hebrew and the words "the LORD." It would seem that "the LORD" is in apposition to the "man" Eve had just brought forth. Consequently, it may be fairly stated that Eve thought that the birth of her first son would be the answer to the promise of Genesis 3:15 and that this male descendant would be divine!

But, some object, Cain was not even in the messianic line. True, but the text only reports what *Eve* thought. She apparently understood that the male offspring promised to her would be no less than a divine-human person. While her instincts were correct, her timing and identifying abilities were not. She must have gotten the idea that one of her sons would be this conquering hero that would vanquish the Serpent. She hoped that relief and correction to her sin would come sooner rather than later.

The second crisis came in the flood that destroyed all mortals on earth except the eight who were in Noah's ark: Noah, his wife, their sons (Shem, Ham, and Japheth), and their sons' wives. But when the eight survivors emerged from the ark, God gave a special promise to Shem (Gen. 9:27)— that God would "dwell in the tents of Shem." This promise to "dwell" was most encouraging, for it assured mortals that despite God's transcendence, he would come to planet earth to take up his residence with the line of Shem, the group of people we know as Semites.

But that left open the question as to which Semite it would be. Would he come from an Arab Semitic line or a Jewish Semitic line? Or would he hail from one of the many other Semitic peoples?

That question was answered only after the third crisis arrived. It came as the Tower of Babel was being built. Once again, the people sought a "name," or a reputation for themselves (cf. Gen. 6:4; 11:4). They sought their unity not in their Creator, but in a tower that would symbolize their own genius.

But the whole project was suddenly interrupted when the Lord intervened, confusing their language so they were no longer able to communicate with each other. Curiously, when they dropped their conversation with God to learn what his will and ways were, they simultaneously lost their ability to communicate with each other—a situation that has some strong similarities to our present predicaments.

Once again, for the third time in these early chapters of Genesis, God's antidote for the mess that humanity had managed to concoct, was a promise from God. God chose a Hebrew Semite named Abraham to be his means of bringing the gospel blessing to all of the world. Even though God had revealed his grace all during the millennia of Genesis 1–11, now in Genesis 12:1–3 he would give the most succinct statement of his promise-plan for the ages to come.

Genesis 12:1–3

After each of the successive failures of the fall, the flood, and the flop of the Tower of Babel, our Lord had given a word of grace: Genesis 3:15; 9:27; and now 12:1–3. And whereas God had repeatedly blessed his creation with his word of benediction, now as he introduces this new word of grace in Genesis 12:1–3, he repeats five times his determination to "bless" Abraham, his seed, and all the families of the earth.

Despite this repeated offer in the past, beginning with the word to Adam and Eve, where "he blessed them saying, 'Be fruitful and multiply,'" humanity insisted on seeking meaning on its own terms by questing for a "name." That is why the bold announcement in Genesis 12:2, where God declared that he would give a "name" to Abram, was so unexpected. Rather than it being an achievement that came by means of Abram's own works, it would come as a gift from God's free grace.

How and why God chose Abram is not discussed in the text; the fact is that he did! This son of Terah was commanded by God to leave his city, Ur of the Babylonians, and journey with his herds and flocks to a land God would only later disclose to him. The amazing thing is that Abram picked up all that he owned and left, going by faith and trusting in the fact that God would tell him what he was to do next.

God gave Abram a covenant at that time. It announced:

> "I will make you into a great nation
>   and I will bless you;
>   I will make your name great,
>   So that all the people on earth may be blessed through you.
>   In order that you may be a blessing;
>   I will bless those who bless you,
>   And whoever curses you I will curse.
>   *So that all the people on earth may be blessed through you.*"
>
> (author's translation)

Abram was promised three blessings: (1) that he would be a great nation, (2) that God would personally bless him, and (3) that his "name" would be great. But why would God seek to do this for one isolated individual? The answer came in the fourth clause, which we have translated here as a purpose clause: "*in order that* you may be a blessing." Therefore, this man was not to be singled out as one of God's favorites whom he would spoil rotten with gifts beyond what he should! Everything he was given was a gift to be shared for the enrichment of others. However, it still is not specific enough. How is this to be done and with whom is he to share this?

Two more promises are given in the clauses that follow. They speak of two whole classes of humankind who will make opposite responses to Abram and to the God of Abram: some blessing and others cursing him.

The final purpose clause shifts to the Hebrew perfect tense to summarize the key purpose of the whole covenant of promise that was so surprisingly offered to Abram. It was "so that all the peoples on earth might be blessed through you" (Gen. 12:3).

This promise of a universal blessing to the "peoples" or "families" on earth is repeated in Genesis 18:18; 22:18; 26:4; and 28:14. In Genesis 12:3 and 28:14 the Hebrew phrase used for "all the peoples/families" is *kôl mišpĕḥôt,* a phrase that is rendered in the Greek translation of the Old Testament as *pasai hai phulai,* meaning " all the tribes" in most contexts, but it could also stand for households as in Joshua 7:14.[2] Therefore, the blessing of God given to Abraham was intended to reach smaller people groups as well as the political groupings of nations. The latter point is made clear in the fact that in Genesis 18:18; 22:18; and 26:4 the Hebrew phrase in this identical expression is *kôl gôyê,* "all the nations," which the Greek translated as *panta ta ethnē,* "all the nations." Acts 3:25 used the Greek phrase, *pasai hai patriai,* "all the families." A *patria* is a people group, which is a subgroup of a tribe or a clan. (It can also be congruent with the tribe or clan in its entirety.) But the sweep of all the evidence makes it abundantly clear that God's gift of a blessing through the instrumentality of Abraham was to be experienced by nations, clans, tribes, people groups, and individuals. It would be for every size group, from the smallest people group to the greatest nation.

One of the most hotly contested points in Genesis 12:3, however, is whether the verb "to bless" is to be translated as a passive ("all peoples on earth will be blessed") or as a reflexive ("will bless themselves"). Most recent commentators remain skeptical about the passive rendering of this Hebrew niphal form of the verb "to bless." But what they fail to observe is that already the previous purpose clause, after the first three promises in Genesis 12:2, had stated as much without specifying exactly to whom Abram was to be a blessing. Furthermore, no one has taken up the challenge laid down in 1927 by O. T. Allis on the necessity of translating the niphal as a passive and not as a reflexive.[3] It is not without significance that all five of the Genesis passages recording the Abrahamic promise are rendered as passives in the Samaritan Version, the Babylonian (Onkelos) Targum, the Jerusalem (Pseudo-Jonathan) Targum, and all citations of these references

2. See the fine discussion on these grammatical points in John Piper, *Let the Nations Be Glad! The Supremacy of God in Missions* (Grand Rapids: Baker, 1993), pp. 177–84.

3. See Oswald T. Allis, "The Blessing of Abraham," *Princeton Theological Review* 25 (1927): 263–98. See also Walter C. Kaiser, Jr., *Toward an Old Testament Theology* (Grand Rapids: Zondervan, 1978), pp. 13–14, 30–32, 83, 86–88.

in the intertestamental literature, as well as in the New Testament (e.g., Acts 3:25).

The promise of blessing that is to come from the hand of God (hence the passive form of the verb) stands in opposition to the curse. Whereas the whole created order had been put under a curse because of the sin of Adam and Eve, God's blessing would potentially be just as universal and extensive in its universal application. It would not be a matter of the nations looking over the fence to see what Israel had done and then, in copy-cat fashion, blessing themselves. It would be only by grace, as a gift of God— not by works. This would be the basis for God's blessing humanity in personal salvation.

The apostle Paul had named Abraham (the later, changed form of his name Abram) as "heir of the world" (Rom. 4:13) and later in Galatians as the father of all who believe in Christ (Gal. 3:29). In fact, the word given in Genesis 12:3 that in Abraham's seed all the nations of the earth would be blessed is equated with the sum and substance of the "gospel" in Galatians 3:8. Therefore, without a doubt we are at the center of what is at the core of the gospel and mission in both Testaments.

The nations were to be blessed in this man's "seed." Accordingly, the "seed" of the woman (Gen. 3:15), the "seed" of Shem in whose tents God would "dwell" (Gen. 9:27), and the "seed" of Abraham formed one collective whole. That one "Seed" was epitomized through its succession of representatives who acted as earnests or down payments until Christ himself should come in that same line of representatives as both part of that succession and as the final consummation of that to which it pointed. Moreover, all who believed, in all ages, were likewise part of the many of whom the One, Christ, embodied the collective whole. The word to Abraham was meant to have a great impact on all the families on the face of the earth in all ages: a high and lofty missionary teaching, if there ever was one.

The whole purpose of God was to bless one people so that they might be the channel through which all the nations on the earth might receive a blessing. Israel was to be God's missionaries to the world—and thereby so are all who believe in this same gospel.

Meanwhile the quest for a name, a reputation, and fame goes on in Israel as it does in the world today, down playing God's offer of a special name to all who will believe and become part of the family of Abraham and of God.

Even if all of the above argument is agreed to in our day, many will still claim that Abraham and his successors did not have anything like a missionary mandate to be actively involved in spreading the Good News. The thought is that God was the only actor on the scene and the Old Testament saints were assigned a role in the cosmic order that was only meant to be *passive*. This leads us to our next text that refutes that claim even more explicitly.

Moses' Encounter with Pharaoh

The events of the exodus from Egypt are remarkable in that they repeatedly focus on the fact that everything that is happening to the Egyptians and to Pharaoh in particular has an evangelistic thrust to it! Almost a dozen and a half times in Scripture the reason that is given for the plagues and the crossing of the Red Sea is that they are not simply to eradicate the Egyptians or their king, but so that "the Egyptians will know that I am the LORD" (Exod. 7:5, 17; 8:22; 14:4, 18). It is stated even more strenuously in Exodus 9:14, 16:

> [T]his time I will send the full force of my plagues against you and against your officials and your people, so that you may know that there is no one like me in all the earth. . . . But I have raised you up for this very purpose that I might show you my power and that my name might be proclaimed in all the earth.

There can be little mistaking the fact that the word "know" here connotes more than a mere cognitive awareness of who God is. It expresses a desire that the Egyptians might themselves come to a personal and experiential knowledge of who Yahweh is. God would proclaim his own name among the Gentiles even if the Israelites were not outgoing in their witness.

Should the question be raised as to the effectiveness of all these demonstrations of the power of God in the plagues and the crossing of the Red Sea, the answer is available to us. When Israel left Egypt, "a "mixed multitude" or a group of "many other peoples" went out with them (Exod. 12:38). This would seem to indicate that many Egyptians were more than merely impressed by what they saw and heard. They were some of the firstfruits of the work of God in their midst. Given the background of the Egyptian religion with all of the gods symbolized by the very elements that were hit by the plagues, it would seem fair to say that the plagues announced Yahweh's victory over the power of the occultic religion of Egypt.

The point that Moses wanted Pharaoh and the people of Egypt to understand through the plagues was that they might "know that all the earth is the LORD's" (Exod. 9:29). The idols of Egypt, as in every other nation, cult, or religion, were no match for the One and only Living God!

Indeed, many of "those officials of Pharaoh who feared the word of the LORD hurried to bring their slaves and their livestock inside. But those who ignored the word of the LORD left their slaves and livestock in the field" during the plague of the hail (Exod. 9:20–21). To "fear the word of the LORD" was to believe in him and to act on the basis of what he had said. Salvation was coming to the Gentiles because they responded obediently to the word of God.

Exodus 19:4–6

The election of Israel, far from meaning the rejection of the other nations of the world, was the very means of salvation of the nations. Election was not a call to privilege, but a choosing for service. As such, the priestly character of the nation of Israel came into view almost from the beginning of her existence as a nation. The people were to be God's ministers, his preachers, his prophets to their own nation as well as to the other nations.

In Moses' famous "Eagle's Wings Speech" beginning in Exodus 19:3, God reviews how he had led Israel to that point in time. He had borne them like an eagle would work with her young while they were learning to fly. As a consequence of so miraculous a deliverance and an evidence of the grace of God, the text pointedly enjoined, "Now therefore . . ." (Exod. 19:5). In light of the grace of God, the text goes on to say,

> if you will obey me fully and keep my covenant, then out of all the nations you will be my treasured possession. Although the whole earth is mine, you will be to me a kingdom of priests and a holy nation. (Exod. 19:5–6)

Three ministries are specified for the nation Israel. First, they were to be God's "treasured possession." The older English versions have "my peculiar people," coming from the Latin word meaning "property," "cattle," "one's own." The Hebrew word *sĕgullâ*[4] referred to property that could be moved as opposed to real estate that could not be moved. Accordingly, Israel was to be God's "jewels" (as noted in Mal. 3:17), his special treasure above all his other possessions. But they were to be treasures that he could move around and disperse as he pleased.

---

4. See Kaiser, *Old Testament Theology,* pp. 105–7, for a discussion on *sĕgullâ.*

A second role that Israel was to play was that of being a "kingdom of priests" to God. This phrase is best translated as "kings and priests,"[5] or royal priests to God. Here is where Israel's role and function on behalf of the kingdom of God is made explicit if it was ambiguous previously. Her role as a nation was a mediatorial role as they related to the nations and people groups around them.

It was this passage that became the basis for the famous New Testament doctrine of the priesthood of believers (1 Peter 2:9; Rev. 1:6; 5:10). Unfortunately for Israel, when this ministry for all the believers was opened to them in this Eagle's Wings Speech, they turned back from so awesome a task. Instead, they urged Moses to go Mount Sinai on their behalf to get the word of God, for they felt both unworthy and too frightened to stand in the presence of so holy a God to receive the word of God directly and personally. But what was rejected at this moment was never disposed of, but simply delayed in its fullest expression until New Testament times. It was not scrapped: it remained God's plan for believers.

A third function was proffered to the nation: they were to be a "holy nation." This meant that they were to be "wholly" the Lord's. It is a shame that we divided the words in English and made "holy" a religious term and "wholly" a secular term. The truth is that the Old Testament word "holy" meant "*set apart wholly* for God's use." This nation was to be set apart not only in their lives, but also in their service. Through them all the families of the earth were to receive the blessing God had in store for all who believed.

As God's special moveable treasure, his royal priests, and a nation wholly dedicated to him, Israel was to assume two relations: one side toward God, their King, and the other side toward the nations and people groups on earth. They were to be a nation for all times and for all peoples—distinctly marked and challenged to serve. Alas, however, Israel missed the prize of her high calling and acted selfishly on her own behalf only. Thus, while carrying a portfolio of the coming Man of Promise and the Seed by which all the world would be blessed, she myopically declined, for the most part, to carry out her high calling as the channel through which the grace of God could come to all the nations.

Of course, other peoples beyond Israel were to share in this joyous service of ministering to all the peoples on earth; *all* who believed in the Old Testament times, whether they were Jewish or not, and all who believed in the church were just as much a part of Abraham's "seed" (Gal. 3:29). This is not to blur the distinction between Israel and the church, for even though

5. Ibid., pp. 107–10, for a discussion on kingly priests.

there is only one "people of God" in both Testaments, it is still possible to distinguish the two just as one can distinguish between male and female, slave and free, or Jew and Gentile. But the apostle Paul's argument was that despite our ability to make these distinctions, the middle wall of partition between believers, regardless of which one of these groups they belonged to, no longer made any difference in Christ (Gal. 3:28; Eph. 2:14). All who believe are one in the Messiah: Jewishness, femaleness, maleness, Gentileness, and slave status no longer marked believers off from one another.

The "people of God" in all ages have been one. Together they have all been called to the same privilege of service and ministry on behalf of the coming Man of Promise. All were to be agents of God's blessing to all on earth. Nothing could be clearer from the missionary and ministry call issued in Exodus 19:4–6.

The Mosaic Legislation on the Sojourner and Foreigner

Careful provisions and instructions were given concerning the "resident alien" (Hebrew: *gēr*) in the Mosaic legislation. Moses taught: "Do not mistreat an alien or oppress him, for you were aliens in Egypt" (Exod. 22:21; Lev. 19:33). But even more significantly, "an alien living among you who wants to celebrate the LORD's Passover must have all the males in his household circumcised; then he may take part like one born in the land" (Exod. 12:48; Num. 9:14). Accordingly, it is not an outlandish idea to think that the Lord was simultaneously extending the offer of salvation to others during the Old Testament era in addition to Israel.

It was for this reason that Solomon prayed during his dedicatory prayer for the temple in the same manner:

> As for the foreigner who does not belong to your people Israel
> but who has come from a distant land because of your name—
> for men will hear of your great name and your mighty hand and
> your outstretched arm—when he comes and prays toward this
> temple, then hear from heaven, your dwelling place, and do
> whatever the foreigner asks of you, so that all the peoples of
> the earth may know your name and fear you, as do your own
> people Israel. (1 Kings 8:41–43)

Foreigners and Gentiles were expected to come to worship the Living God because of the nature, power, and saving qualities of the Name of

God. It was expected that God would hear and respond to their prayers just as effectively as he would listen to and answer the prayers of Israelites. Indeed, God was Lord over all the earth. This is why the psalmist will later invite all the nations of all the earth to join in worshiping of the One and only God of all the universe.

2 Samuel 7

To complete our study of the plan of God for the peoples of the earth, it is necessary to investigate the continuation of the promise first made to Eve, Shem, Abraham, Isaac, and Jacob, but now announced to David in 2 Samuel 7. Next in importance to the promise given to Eve and Abraham must rank the promise given to David. Here was the next expansion of that same plan. It is recorded twice in Scripture—2 Samuel 7 and 1 Chronicles 17—and a commentary on it is given in Psalm 89.

It had always been in the plan of God to give to the nation of Israel a king. Moses had promised that as far back as in Deuteronomy 17:14–20. But in the interim, several usurpers had surfaced prematurely, attempting to shortcircuit the timing of God. Gideon was one of the first to receive an offer to "rule over" the men of Israel (Judg. 8:22). Whereas he declined the offer, his son Abimelech jumped at the opportunity and the result was a tragedy (Judg. 9:15–18). Neither was Samuel's generation any wiser, for they also asked for a king prematurely (1 Sam. 8:4–6). The problem was not with the request for a king, but with the motivation that triggered it: they wanted to have a king so they could be "like the other nations." Graciously God yielded to their request and indeed Saul had marvelous success his first twenty years or so (1 Sam. 14:47). But after he turned away from the Lord, the Lord turned away from him.

It was at this point that the Lord called David to be king in place of Saul. After David had been given rest from all his enemies, he built a cedar palace for himself. It was at the open house for the new palace that David remarked in an off-handed manner to the prophet Nathan that it was his desire to build a new house for God as well. To this Nathan responded positively with his own human approval of the idea (2 Sam. 7:2). However, that night the Lord appeared to the prophet Nathan with the divine word that David was not to build the temple for God since his hands were full of the blood of the wars he had fought.

But there was a compensating word from God to David. God promised to make a "house," that is, a dynasty, out of David (v. 11). Moreover, the

"Seed," to whom David looked and trusted for his salvation, would now "come from [David's] own body" (v. 12). God would also grant him a throne and a kingdom that would last forever (v. 16).

It was in the midst of all of these surprise announcements that the overwhelmed David went in, sat before the Lord, and exclaimed,

> Who am I, O Lord Yahweh,
> and who is my family,
> that you have brought me this far?
> And as if this is not enough in your sight, O Lord Yahweh,
> You have spoken about the future of the house of your servant.
> And this is the charter for humanity, O Lord Yahweh.
>
> (author's translation; 2 Sam. 7:18–19)

There are a number of unusual things about these verses. One notices immediately the use of "Adonai Yahweh," "Lord Yahweh," for a total of five times in verses 18–19, 22, 28–29. R. A. Carlson had noticed that this unique compound name had been used previously when God had promised Abraham a "seed" in Genesis 15:2, 8. It occurs in other books only seven times, but never again in Samuel.[6] Its repeated use in 2 Samuel 7 with the Davidic covenant of promise and in Genesis 15 with the Abrahamic promise is too striking to be accidental and without special reason: the two covenants were thereby drawn into the closest of relationships.

But that is all the more reason why we must pay attention to the phrase "charter for humanity" in 2 Samuel 7:19. What was this *tôrâ*, "law," or "charter" that was for all humanity? First, this translation is to be preferred to the completely incorrect rendering in most English versions that say something like the NIV's "Is this your usual way of dealing with man?"[7] That rendering is miles away from what the Hebrew expression meant. It was instead the "outline," "law," or even "decree" by which God estab-

---

6. R. A. Carlson, *David the Chosen King: A Traditio-Historical Approach to the Second Book of Samuel,* trans. Eric Sharpe and Stanley Rudman (Stockholm: Almqvist and Wiksell, 1964), p. 127. The seven other instances are Deut. 3:24; 9:26; Josh. 7:7; Judg. 6:22;16:28; 1 Kings 2:26; 8:53.

7. See Kaiser, *Toward an Old Testament Theology,* pp. 152–55 and the quote there from Henri Cazelles, "Review of Roland deVaux's *Les Institutiones de L'ancien Testament,*" *Vetus Testamentum* 8 (1958): 322, and idem, "Shiloh, the Customary Laws and the Return of Ancient Kings," in *Proclamation and Presence,* ed. John T. Durham and J. R. Porter (Richmond: John Knox, 1970), p. 250, where Cazelles pointed to the parallel Akkadian term *terit nishe,* which he translated as "qui fixe le destin des hommes," or "the decree concerning humanity in general."

lished his plan for all of humanity. Once again, at the most critical point of the gospel, not only have we moderns failed to hear the most significant point of all, but also have muted it with our own translations. The gospel was indeed a chapter on teaching for all humankind and not just for Israel.

However, David had not missed this point. He realized that he had just been given an everlasting dynasty, dominion, and kingdom, which was all linked with the ongoing promise that God had been announcing repeatedly. The ancient plan of God would continue, but as usual, it would involve the future of all humanity! Surely that is missions at its highest watermark!

And what did David have reference to by his use of "this" in "and this is the charter for humanity"? The antecedent can be nothing less than the substance of the oracle that had just been given to him by the prophet Nathan. "This" refers in context to the revelation David had just been given about the "seed."

Tôrâ cannot be rendered, as it is in so many modern versions of the last centuries, as "custom," "manner," or "estate." There are good Hebrew words for all of those concepts. But *tôrâ* here means "teaching," for it comes from the root *yārâ*, which means "to direct," "to teach," "to instruct."[8] Consequently, we have rendered it something like a "charter/ teaching for humanity."

And that is what God granted to David and to the nations of the earth. It was not a "law for Adam," for there is no reference to Adam or to a covenant being made with him. Nor can it be rendered "the law of the Man," that is, the Lord God, for such a usage is unknown up to this era and none subsequently refer back to it with such an ideology.

Therefore, we are left with instruction that has relevance for all humanity. What God had earlier given to Abraham, Isaac, and Jacob, he had now continued through David.

Conclusion

The plan of God had from the very beginning the central figure of the "Seed" who was to come in the person of the Man of Promise, the Messiah. It was a message aimed universally at all people groups and nations

8. See Walter C. Kaiser, Jr., "The Blessing of David: A Charter for Humanity," in *The Law and the Prophets,* ed. John Skilton (Philadelphia: Presbyterian & Reformed, 1974), pp. 298–318.

from the very beginning. We do not, as David Filbeck claimed, move from the universalism of Genesis 1–11 to the particularism later in Israel at the time of the giving of the Law, back to an emerging universal offer of the gospel once again in time of the kingdom and the prophets.[9] Instead, it was ever and always the plain offer of God to all the peoples of the earth through his elected servants of the promise-plan.

9. David Filbeck, *Yes, God of the Gentiles, Too: The Missionary Message of the Old Testament* (Wheaton, Ill.: Billy Graham Center, Wheaton College, 1994), p. 75.

TWO

God's Purpose for Missions in the Old Testament

"THE PSALTER is one of the greatest missionary books in the world," taught George Peters. He was correcting Robert Martin-Achard's statement that "it is by reason of [the Psalter] belonging to the realm of creation and not because they are called to share Israel's faith, that the heathen must glorify God."[1] Peters retorted:

> This, however, is only relatively true. It is a profound fact that "the hymn of praise is missionary preaching par excellence," especially when we realize that such missionary preaching is supported in the Psalms by more than 175 references of a universalistic note relating to the nations of the world. Many of them bring hope of salvation to the nations. . . . Indeed, the Psalter is one of the greatest missionary books in the world, though seldom seen from that point of view.[2]

Peters went on to say that all the psalms could be labeled as missionary psalms with direct missionary messages and challenges. Peters then listed

1. Robert Martin-Achard, *A Light to the Nations: A Study of the Old Testament Conception of Israel's Mission to the World* (London: Oliver & Boyd, 1962), p. 58.

2. George Peters, *A Biblical Theology of Missions* (Chicago: Moody, 1972), pp. 115–16.   29

Psalms 2, 33, 66, 72, 98, 117, and 145.[3] But why did Peters fail to mention Psalms 67, 96, and 100? We would like to correct that oversight by focusing first on Psalm 67.

Psalm 67

This psalm has often been called the "Old Testament *Pater Noster*," the "Our Father" psalm. It is also the psalm that focuses on the promise made to Abraham that he would be a blessing to all the families of the earth. As Derek Kidner observed, "If a psalm was ever written around the promises to Abraham, that he would be both blessed and made a blessing, it could well have been such as [Psalm 67]."[4]

But if the subject of the psalm is the Abrahamic promise, one of its key texts from the informing theology of antecedent Scripture is the Aaronic benediction from Numbers 6:24–26.

> The LORD [=Yahweh] bless you and keep you;
> The LORD [=Yahweh] make his face shine upon you
> And be gracious to you;
> The LORD [=Yahweh] turn his face toward you
> And give you peace.

These are the words often heard at the close of many Christian worship services, but look how the psalmist employs them here. Rather than saying Yahweh (=LORD), the covenantal and personal name used by those who have an intimate relationship to God, the psalmist substituted *Elohim* ("God"), the name used when one must express the Lord's relationship to all people, nations, and creation. The psalmist also prayed, "May God be gracious to us and bless us," thereby changing, ever so slightly, the object from the second-person pronoun "you" to the first-person plural "us."

It is worth noting that this same Aaronic formula appears in Psalm 4:6 (7), Psalm 31:16 (17), and a thrice-repeated refrain in Psalm 80:3, 7, 19. All these psalms borrowed from the earlier benediction in Numbers 6:24–26.

The psalm is marked off into three distinct strophes, or poetic paragraphs, each using the rhetorical device in verses 3 and 5 of the repeated

---

3. Ibid., p. 116.
4. Derek Kidner, *A Commentary on the Psalms,* 2 vols. (Downers Grove, Ill.: InterVarsity, 1971), 1:236.

phrase ("May all the peoples praise you, O God; may all the peoples praise you") to indicate the end of the strophe. The structure is almost an exact replica of Genesis 12:2–3—Bless us . . . bless us . . . bless us . . . so that all the nations might come to know the Lord.

It is interesting to note that the psalmist has directly applied what the high priest Aaron and his fellow priests bestowed on the nation Israel to all the peoples and nations on earth. It is from this theme enlargement that we boldly announce that this is indeed a missionary psalm. Nor can it escape our attention that the purpose for this enlarged blessing upon all the nations of the world is specifically so "that your ways may be known on earth, your salvation among all nations" (Ps. 67:2). That is why God had been gracious to Israel and had blessed them in such an extraordinary manner. With that conclusion, Genesis 12:3b is in full agreement.

The very bounty of God would be reason enough for the peoples of the earth to sit up and take notice that indeed their God was God alone and able to work far beyond what could be attributed to human ability or genius. Therefore, the sentiment of Psalm 67 is this: May God be gracious and bless us fellow Israelites. May he increase our families, making them large and spiritually prosperous. May our crops increase and produce bountifully and our flocks show marked enlargement. May all of this and more happen so that the nations may look on us and say that what Aaron prayed for, by way of God's blessing, has indeed occurred. The very bounty of God demonstrates that God has blessed us. Accordingly, may the rest of God's purpose come to pass as well, that in the blessing of Israel all the nations of the earth might be drawn to receive the message of God's salvation as well.

It is not without significance that this psalm was sung at the Feast of Pentecost. When one remembers that it was at the Feast of Pentecost that God was to pour out his Spirit on all flesh, just as the prophet Joel had predicted (Joel 2:28–31), the connection of this psalm with the Feast of Pentecost and its missionary message is all the more remarkable. The Feast of Pentecost came at the time of the ingathering of the previous year's harvest. Thus, the psalmist sees the ingathering of the crops as an earnest, a down payment, and a symbol of the spiritual harvest that God desired for every tribe, tongue, and nation. So may the Lord himself be gracious (i.e., full of grace) to all of us and bless us through that repeated word of promise he had given to Abraham in Genesis 12:3.

The psalmist calls us to prove and test God's purposes for three reasons. These three reasons fit into the three strophes already observed as the structure used here and probably directly imitating the structure of Genesis 12:2–3.

The first reason Israel and all believers are called to prove God's purpose to bless all the nations is because God has been so gracious to us (vv. 1–3). The wish that God would continue to prosper and grant his favor on the nation of Israel was not to be better than others or to get ahead of the other nations. The purpose infinitive of verse 2 instead said it was specifically so that all the nations might come to know the "ways" of God "on earth." God's goodness to Israel would happily lead, so the wish intended, to a recognition of God among the heathen as Lord of all. God's "way" (literally) was his purpose of grace, his salvation that was intended not just for Israel, but for the whole world.

Accordingly, God had not blessed Israel and been kind to them because they were his pets, his favorites, or because his grace was limited to them for the period of the Old Testament. Instead, God's mode of dealing with Israel was to communicate to them a message that they in turn were responsible for disseminating to all the peoples of the earth.

The strophe and this first reason end with an invitation to all the peoples of the world to join in praising so wonderful a Savior who has worked all things out so well:

> May the peoples praise you, O God;
> May all the peoples praise you.

It is clear that the intent of the psalm is that God might be praised and that this doxology must be offered by all the peoples of the world. Doxology is not an optional feature of human life. Nor is it the requirement solely of those who know this Lord and who are believers. Every creature on planet earth, regardless of their religious or nonreligious preferences, must give glory and praise to this God. He is the One who made them and he is the One they will all one day face.

To this is added a second reason: because God rules and guides all nations (vv. 4–5). He is not a judge in the judicial, condemning sense, but a royal ruler who rules in righteousness. He is a shepherd of the nations just as the Great Shepherd in Psalm 23:3 is depicted. He will reign, as Psalm 72 promised, wherever the sun sojourns. If this God is not limited to the territory of the nation Israel, where he is currently being worshiped, and if he has power over all the earth, then there is all the more reason why he should be acknowledged as Lord and Savior of all the peoples on the earth. So let us join in the refrain once again in worship of so sovereign a Lord.

A third and final reason is given: because of the very goodness of God (vv. 6–7). God called Israel, and hence all believers, to prove his purpose to bless the nations simply because he had been so good to the nation. Certainly the land had yielded its overwhelming increase and the grain bins and storage areas were filled to overflowing. Was this not evidence that God had answered the prayer of Aaron and the priests recorded in Numbers 6:24–26?

The question ought to have stunned every Israelite: Why has God blessed them so abundantly? Once again it is best to render the final clause in verse 7 as a purpose or result clause: "so that all the ends of the earth might fear him." No other reason will satisfy the extraordinary evidence of the power of God at work.

But the point must not be lost in the shuffle: the same power and presence of God that had brought material increase was now available for the spiritual increase that would visit all the nations and peoples on earth. The psalmist was not just mouthing empty words or hyping pious-sounding concepts that no one expected anyone to do anything about it. The psalmist and the revealing word of God expected the people of Israel to experience a real change in their lives. He wanted them to be the agents through which the blessing of God would come to all the peoples on earth. That was the only way they could join in the refrain and fulfill the prayer and wish that "all the peoples might praise" God as their God too.

This purpose for Israel as a missionary force originated in the universal scope of the message in Genesis 1–11 and more definitively in Genesis 12:3. But it would achieve its clearest definition in the "Servant of the Lord" passages in Isaiah 42 and 49, where Israel, who was also that "servant," was appointed to be "a light to the nations."

God wanted the nations to come to "fear" him. The word "fear" here did not mean terror or fright, for there were two antonymic usages of the word "fear." Exodus 20:20 illustrated the two usages in the same verse: "Fear not, but rather fear the LORD." Therefore, it urged, do not be frightened or scared; instead, put your whole trust and faith in the Lord. In this latter sense, then, the fear of the Lord is the beginning of everything: of understanding, of living, of personal holiness, of a personal relationship with the Living God. This is what the goodness of God was driving Israel to: a key way to bring all the nations on planet earth to believe in him. Therefore, Israel was to be a witnessing, proclaiming, and evangelizing nation. The Gentiles just had to be brought to the light!

Psalm 96

Psalm 96 is another of the great missionary psalms, for the anonymous author orders the Jewish audience not only to "Sing to the LORD," but to "proclaim his salvation day after day. Declare his glory among the nations, his marvelous deeds among all peoples" (Ps. 96:2–3).

Clearly the content is Good News and salvation. The extent of this declaration is also clear: among all the nations and among all the peoples.

The Hebrew word for "proclaim" (Hebrew root of *bśr; bāśar*)[5] is the Old Testament equivalent of the New Testament *euangelizomai,* "to bring good news," "to announce glad tidings," or "to announce the gospel." As most know, the "announcement of good news" in the New Testament is applied to the finished work of Christ on the cross. And here it is expressly applied to the call to announce this same news about the Messiah to the nations and peoples of the world. Surely this is what missions are all about.

Some may be tempted to conclude that this psalm is purely eschatological, but that flies in the face of verse 5, which is pivotal for this psalm. W. Creighton Marlowe makes the point that "the psalm is unmistakable in its sentiment that all nations ought to know [Yahweh] and make Him known. It despoils the polytheism of the ancient Near East."[6] Marlowe went on, in that same context, to show how the psalmist employs a marvelous pun here.

"Above all gods" in v. 4 and similar statements elsewhere in the OT raise the question "does the OT assume the existence of other gods?" That the answer is no is demonstrated in v. 5, where the term "idols" is *elilim,* an intensive plural of a word meaning "nothing"; so the psalmist says the so-called gods are really "the greatest nothings of all" (cf. Heb. *'elohim*).

The context demands that God's character ("glory") and his conduct ("deeds") be "declared" (Hebrew: *spr*) universally and internationally (v. 3). The psalm goes on to address all the "families of nations" (v. 7) and instructs them to "ascribe glory to the LORD" and to bring sacrifices and worship into his courts. This is not an exclusively Israelite privilege; "all the earth" is to "tremble before him" (v. 9).

5. W. Creighton Marlowe, "The Music of Missions: Themes of Cross-Cultural Outreach in the Psalms," *Missiology* 26 (1998): 456, n. 33, notes that *bśr* appears also in Ps. 40:9 (10) and Ps. 68:11 (12). It also appears in important eschatological and soteriological texts such as Isa. 40:9; 41:27; 52:7; and 61:1.

6. Marlowe, "Music of Missions," 455.

Israel, along with the new converts from all the earth, are to "preach" (Hebrew: *'āmar*) that "Yahweh reigns" and that he will come to "judge the peoples with equity" (v. 10).

The command to "declare" (Hebrew: *spr*) is used only here in the psalms in the imperative form of the intensive stem of the verb. Though not in the imperative form, the same verb occurs in Psalm 2:7, where God says of his Son, the Messiah, "I will declare the decree of the LORD," an investiture formula that goes on to announce, "You are my Son, today I have begotten you." Thus, despite the international rebellion against God and his Son's program, the nations must come to reckon with the fact that they will be subject to the judgment of God by the hand of his Son if they do not come to terms with him in belief (Ps. 2:9–12). Once again, the implication is that an active proclamation of the Good News exists for all the nations to respond.

Likewise, Psalm 9 uses the verb *spr,* to "declare" (v. 1 [2]) with another verb, "to make known, tell" (Hebrew: *ngd;* v. 11 [12]). The psalm begins with a declaration that the congregation will sing praises to the Lord. At the pivotal spot in the psalm, once again, verses 7–8 (8–9) declare that "Yahweh reigns, for he has established his throne for judgment. He will judge the world in righteousness."

The final realization of this psalm waits until the end day of Messiah's second coming, but not everything in the psalm is to be postponed until then. The injunction to "proclaim among the nations what [Yahweh] has done" (v. 11 [12]) is not reserved for the eschaton, for the reason given in the next verse indicates that Yahweh is currently in the business of providing refuge and relief from the foes who oppose his people.

Thus, praise of God preceded preaching, but both were part and parcel of Israel's witness to the nations. The point is that there was a call for an *active* witness (i.e., it was to be centrifugal in its effect, reaching out from the center to others) by Israel to the Gentiles.

Other psalms call for the same active and centrifugal outreach on the part of Israel:

"I will make confession [Hebrew: *ydh*] about you, O Yahweh,
    I will sing to you among the nations" (57:9).

"I will speak of your statutes before kings" (Ps. 119:46).

"Our mouths were filled with laughter,
    our tongues with songs of joy.
Then it was said among the nations,
    "The LORD has done great things for them" (126:2–3).

"They will tell of the glory of your kingdom
and speak of your might,
so that all men may know of your mighty acts
and the splendor of your kingdom" (145:11–12).

"My mouth will speak in praise of the LORD.
Let every creature praise his holy name for ever and ever" (145:21).

Psalm 117

While this psalm is not as explicit a missionary psalm as Psalms 67 and 96, nevertheless, it does call for extolling the Name of God before all the nations and all the peoples.

The international Gentile people groups (Hebrew: *gôyîm* // *ʿammîm*) must be told of the loyal faithfulness of Yahweh. Accordingly, when all the peoples of the earth are called to praise and extol the Lord, the assumption is that someone has transmitted to them the knowledge and worship of the Living God. But if it is not assumed that the witnesses are Israel, then to whom does the task fall in these days of Old Testament revelation?

The assumption is that the Gentile nations have heard and must continue to do so. How will they be able to respond to the requirement laid on them in this, the briefest of all the psalms, unless Israel has fulfilled her task of sharing the Good News with them?

What would motivate Israel to be so magnanimous unless it was the loyal love and faithfulness (Hebrew: *ḥesed*) of God? This served as Israel's highest motivator for outreach to the Gentiles. Israel's songs of praise, her confession of the wonderful deeds of God on her behalf, and her declaration of the same to the nations was driven solely by the everlasting loyal love and faithfulness of God. Only redeemed Gentiles and Jews can praise God, hence the necessity of active missions in the Old Testament.

Conclusion

It is all too easy to conclude that the Old Testament does not set forth a missionary mandate for Israel since, as George Peters claimed, "Nowhere in the Old Testament was Israel 'sent' to the nations."[7] But Peters linked the word "send" with the New Testament's definition of missions. There-

---

7. Peters, *Biblical Theology of Missions,* p. 21.

fore he unnecessarily eliminated other, legitimate indications of the concept of missions from the older Testament.

Despite that nuanced meaning Peters identified, he nevertheless did find a missionary purpose and theology in the Old Testament. That is why it is not difficult to see how generalizations that deny that any Israelite was ever sent as a missionary to anyone else, or that the Old Testament is totally built around a centripetal emphasis, can find little usefulness in a discussion of God's call for Israel to be a light to the nations. Even though the radical centripetal approach does recognize a certain universality in the Old Testament, which is viewed as foundational for the New Testament call to evangelize, the case laid out here sees more than a mere foundational basis in the Old Testament evangel and its call for Israel's involvement.

Over and over again the psalmists called on all the peoples of all the lands and nations to praise the Lord (Pss. 47:1; 67:3, 5; 100:1; 117:1). Even more directly, these ancient singers of Israel urged their people to tell, proclaim, and make known the mighty deeds of Yahweh (Pss. 9:11; 105:1) and to join in singing praises to God from all the nations (Pss. 18:49; 96:2–3). The psalmists themselves offer to sing God's praises among the nations (Pss. 57:9; 108:3). The expected result would be that all the ends of the earth would turn to the Lord and all the families on earth would bow down in worship to him (Pss. 22:27; 66:4; 86:9).

This is not so surprising, for had not King Solomon in his dedicatory prayer of the temple pronounced a blessing on the people, all the while asking God to bless them in order that all the peoples of the earth might know that Yahweh is God alone (1 Kings 8:43–60)? While some may once again argue that since there was no evidence of a going out or a "sending" to the nations in the form of a missionary, and that missions in the Old Testament are at best centripetal (inward-moving to the center, to Zion) rather than centrifugal (outward-going from the center), we beg to differ with them.

It might be noted, in this connection, that when Jesus cleansed the temple and drove out the money changers, he drove them out of the Court of the Gentiles. Could it be that the concern for commerce in that day had crowded out the requisite concern for the Gentile nations?[8]

The example of Jonah refutes the alleged case for a centripetal-only emphasis in the Old Testament. Jonah was commanded to go preach in the capital city of Assyria, Nineveh. This ministry, even though carried out under considerable duress and a narrow nationalism, was still blessed

---

8. A suggestion made to me in a written communication from Dr. Kenneth Mulholland.

by God. True, Jonah was distressed that God's grace should have been extended to such brutal and hostile enemies who had wrecked so much havoc on Jonah's own homeland. But the fact remains, as we shall see in a later chapter, that Jonah is an excellent example of cross-cultural missions. Therefore, God did send messengers with his message just as the psalmists envisioned. After all, no one thinks up the gospel by himself or herself; it always comes from the outside. That is why it is most difficult to urge Gentiles to extol, praise, and worship Yahweh if they have never been told about his person or work. And this expectation was not reserved only for the eschaton, but was already operative in the days of these singers in Israel. This can be ascertained from the accompanying reasons that appear with the injunctions for all the nations to know the Lord and to serve him. Missions cannot be an afterthought for the Old Testament: it is the heart and core of the plan of God.

THREE

God's Use of Individuals to Reach Gentiles in the Old Testament

WE HAVE argued that Genesis 12:1–3 is foundational to the missionary vision of the whole Bible and the people of God through all the ages. This promise that God would bless "all the families of the earth" is repeated in various forms in Genesis 18:18; 22:18; 26:4; and 28:14. The Hebrew phrase for "all the families" is *kôl mišpĕḥôt,* which is rendered in the Greek translation of the Old Testament in Genesis 12:3 and 28:14 by *pasai hai phulai,* "all the tribes." But the Hebrew word family is used for even smaller groups than "tribes," as it is in the Achan story in Joshua 7:14. Remember that after Achan had sinned, Israel was called forward for examination before God by "tribes," and then by *mišpĕḥôt,* "families," a unit smaller than tribes.

Therefore, we contend that God's promise to Abraham had both a larger and a smaller scope in mind. Indeed, the promise to Abraham envisioned "all the nations" (Hebrew: *kôl gôyê*), which the Septuagint rendered in Genesis 18:18; 22:1; and 26:4 as *panta ta ethnē,* "all the nations." The word for nations *(gôyîm)* was also the word for the "Gentiles." Therefore, it could not be claimed, as is so often the case, that the gospel message in the Old Testament times was exclusively for the Jewish people and the nation of Israel. The "nations" and "Gentiles" were envisioned as equal recipients of that same Good News from the very beginning of time along with Israel herself.

Examples of Individual Believing Gentiles

We see, then, that God did encompass all people groups in the promise given to Abraham. But this truth must not blind our eyes to the fact that God likewise called individuals in the Old Testament. There are just too many examples to the contrary to argue against the case for individual Gentiles who were also included in that Abrahamic promise.

Who were these Gentiles in the Old Testament who were benefiting from the outreach of the grace of God? Well, for starters, consider Melchizedek in Genesis 14. He is described as a "king of Salem" and a "priest of God Most High" (Gen. 14:18). This Canaanite blessed Abram "by God Most High, Creator of heaven and earth," and is the one to whom Abram gave a tithe, a tenth of all he had taken as booty, in his rescue of Lot. Where, when, and how had this king and priest, in the midst of a pagan culture, become a true believer in the Man of Promise who was to come? The text does not supply even a hint. Yet few can deny that he was indeed a believer. He is one of many hints in the Old Testament that many Gentile individuals were coming to know the One who would be later called the Messiah, or Jesus.

There were others. Jethro was a "priest of Midian" (Exod. 18:1). His testimony is startling to those who expect so much less of a desert Midianite in the Arabian sands. When Moses returned from Egypt and told his father-in-law everything the Lord had done to Pharaoh and the Egyptians for the sake of Israel, this Midianite priest broke out into paeans of praise to Yahweh, the Name of God reserved for those who had a personal relationship to the Lord. He exclaimed:

Praise be to [Yahweh] the LORD, who rescued you from the hand of the Egyptians and of Pharaoh, and who rescued the people from the hand of the Egyptians. Now I know that [Yahweh] the LORD is greater than all the other gods, for he did this to those who treated Israel arrogantly. (Exod. 18:10–11)

It was then that Jethro brought a burnt offering and other sacrifices to God as Aaron and all the elders of Israel broke bread together and participated in joint worship of the Living God.

Once again, we are baffled. When did Jethro come to know such saving grace? Had Moses shared the Abrahamic promise with him and had he put all his trust in the coming "Seed" of the woman, the "Seed" of Shem and Abraham's line? He must have done so, for there is no other way to account for the results the text affirms so clearly.

To Melchizedek and Jethro can be added the name of Balaam, son of Beor, who lived in Upper Mesopotamia at Pethor, near the River Euphrates in his native land (Num. 22:5). He is even more mysterious, if that is possible, than the other two we have considered. Here was a Gentile with the prophetic gift! Was he a saint or was he a sinner?[1] That question is not answered easily. One thing is sure: he did accurately deliver the word from Yahweh over four times. Indeed, he did come to a bitter and grievous end in his effort apparently to placate his Moabite host (Num. 31:8), but that does not detract from the fact that here was a Gentile who could address God personally in prayer and also give a direct word from God on high to mortals in Moab and Israel alike. God apparently was calling Gentiles to himself while he was calling Israelites.

Consider also Rahab, the prostitute. When she hid the spies she showed that she feared the God of Israel more than she feared the king of Jericho. Her testimony was quite straightforward:

> I know that [Yahweh] the LORD your God has given this land to you. . . . We have heard how [Yahweh] the LORD dried up the water of the Red Sea for you when you came out of Egypt, and what he did to Sihon and Og, the two kings of the Amorites east of the Jordan, whom you completely destroyed. When we heard of it, our hearts melted and everyone's courage failed because of you, for [Yahweh] the LORD your God is God in heaven above and on earth below. (Josh. 2:9–11)

This was saving faith, for Rahab is listed in the heroes of faith chapter (Heb. 11:31). Similarly, James argues that her good work of hiding the spies came from her genuine faith (James 2:25). Thus, her confession that "Yahweh is God" included a confession that she looked forward to the coming Messiah. The God who had promised the land to Israel was the same God who had promised that he would send his Seed, the Messiah. To believe in one part of this promise was to affirm that one believed in all the promise, for how could this one great promise of God be segmented, divided, or

---

1. See Walter C. Kaiser, Jr., "Balaam, Son of Beor, in Light of Deir 'Alla and Scripture: Saint or Soothsayer?" in *Go to the Land I will Show You: Dwight Young Festschrift*, ed. Joseph Coleson and Victor Matthews (Winona Lake, Ind.: Eisenbrauns, 1996), pp. 95–106.

bifurcated into that which was only temporally real and that which was eternal? Too often too many have assumed that this unilateral, unconditional, and eternal covenant of God could be treated in sections with portions relevant for specified periods. The only problem with that view is that nowhere did the text indicate that it could be treated in that manner. And it becomes impossible to understand how on the basis of such simple words that Rahab could have made it into the hall of faith in Hebrews 11.

The same case could be made for Ruth, the Moabite woman. When Boaz, a relative on Naomi's husband's side, found out who this woman was, and the story of her choice to leave her homeland to follow her mother-in-law, he was impressed. He commented: "May the LORD repay you for what you have done. May you be richly rewarded by [Yahweh] the LORD, the God of Israel, under whose wings you have come to take refuge" (Ruth 2:12). In fact, the son she later bore to Boaz was the grandfather of David, in the line of Messiah.

The Missiological Implications of the Healing of Naaman

We now look at one of the most celebrated Old Testament cases of a Gentile conversion. Second Kings 5:1–19a is one of the most highly developed plots with the largest number of characters among the stories associated with the prophet Elisha.[2] However, it is most unusual in that it credits an unnamed Jewish maid with supplying the key witness to a commander of a foreign army in Syria. But that is getting ahead of our story.

The incident recorded here took place sometime around 852–841 B.C. Neither the king of northern Israel nor of Syria is named, but from the context in which the story is set, it is probable that the Israelite king was Joram (also know as Jehoram) and the Syrian king was Ben-Hadad II. The latter years of Jehoram's reign were filled with hostilities originating with the Syrian/Aramean king, probably due to the fact that the ten northern tribes had failed to join in the continual Syro-Assyrian confrontations that had marked most of the sixth decade of the ninth century B.C. For this failure, the Syrians constantly raided the northern kingdom (2 Kings 6:8), culminating in an all-out offensive against Israel (2 Kings 6:24–7:20).

---

2. I am highly beholden to the unusually fine article from my friend Walter A. Maier III, for this section: "The Healing of Naaman in Missiological Perspective," *Concordia Theological Quarterly* 61 (1997): 177–96.

Our story, however, took place during one of those rare times of peace, or at least the relaxation of hostilities.

The focus of the story was Naaman, "commander of the army" of Syria (2 Kings 5:1). That is the term used for an army's highest-ranking officer, as is clear in the case of Phicol (Gen. 21:22), Sisera (1 Sam. 12:9), and Joab (1 Chron. 27:34). But more than this, his epithets were even more impressive: he was "a great man," that is, one of high social standing and importance. Moreover, he was "highly regarded," a term reminiscent of those to whom the king extended his scepter and "lifted up the face." Finally, he was a "valiant man," that is, a man whose wealth, property holdings, and personal valor had distinguished him in the eyes of his peers.

Even more startling is the note in the first verse of this chapter of 2 Kings 5 that "through him Yahweh had given victory to Aram/Syria." The Hebrew writer declares something that surely was not politically correct, even if it was theologically exact: Yahweh, the God of all creation, could, as a matter of fact, have used a pagan enemy to accomplish what he wanted to be done on earth! This, in itself, was enough to set off bells for every provincial and chauvenistic Israelite reader of this text. Could God have used Gentiles, some would instinctively ask? The next thing some will be saying is that God can redeem Gentiles by the same promise given to Israel, other objectors would stingily add. But that is exactly where the narrative is heading!

Naaman had arrived in his career standings, if one could tell from all the accolades and honors that had been attributed to him. Nothing in his life seemed to be troubling him—except one thing: "he had leprosy" (v. 1). Now Naaman's participation in social settings makes it most unlikely that he had Hanson's disease, for the term "leprosy" (Hebrew: *s ūraʿat;* Greek: *lepra*) was used for a number of undiagnosed diseases. True, leprosy normally was designated with the Greek word *elephantiasis,* our English "elephantitis." In the ancient world, leprosy covered a wide range of diseases, just as our modern term "cancer" covers all sorts of diseases we cannot with certainty classify or identify. Therefore, it would appear that Naaman was suffering from a skin disease, which must have been embarrassing for one in his social standing.

In one of the previous Syrian raids on Israel, a "young girl from Israel" (v. 2) had been taken captive back to Aram and given to Naaman's wife to serve her. It was she who bravely sighed out loud, "If only my master would see the prophet who is in Samaria! He would cure him of his leprosy" (v. 3). What was this girl's name? We do not know. Where did she get such advanced theology? Did she not imply that the God the prophet served could heal? And did she not imply that he could heal Gentiles as well? Even one's enemy? And why did she think that Naaman, great as he was, must go and see this prophet in order to be healed? How could she think this when this God had not chosen to release her from her captors? Would this not be an impediment to her faith? Our questions come faster than the answers to them.

Naaman took the girl seriously, for he went to his king and related what the young captive in his household had said. Ben-Hadad II, who was personally out of solutions for his ranking field general, urged that Naaman go. The king of Syria would send a letter of introduction to the king of Israel, the one on whom he had been so recently inflicting so much trouble by his persistent raids. The letter read: "With this letter I am sending my servant Naaman to you so that you may cure him of his leprosy" (v. 6).

That was enough to make the king of Israel boil. "Who does he think I am?" he cried out in his deep consternation. "Am I God? Can I kill and bring back to life? Why does this fellow send someone to me to be cured of his leprosy? See how he is trying to pick a quarrel with me!" (v. 7).

Given the state of relations between the two countries, one can hardly blame the Israelite king for coming to the conclusion that he reached. Since no mention was made of the witness of the captured maiden, an awkward matter in and of itself, and no mention was made of the prophet in this Israelite capital city, the king presumed that he was supposed to come up with the miracle cure. Odd it is, but at the same time revealing, that poor Israelite maidens and now Syrian generals know what those who have the word of God close at hand did not know: there was a prophet of God in their midst! How sad for Israel that her leaders did not know where to turn in crises like this! Should the king of Israel not have thought of the power of God and the resident prophet of God before he thought of international political intrigue? But such was the state of spiritual affairs among the so-called people of God in those days.

The prophet Elisha heard that the king had torn his robes (v. 8), so he sent an inquiry to the king asking what was the matter. But he also added, "Have the man come to me and he will know that there is a prophet in Israel" (v. 8). Apparently, God had already revealed to his prophet what had caused the king's deep consternation—evidence that nothing is hidden from God as well as the fact that God can reveal even the most intimate details to his prophet.

Advised where to go, Naaman proceeded to go to the prophet's house in Samaria, expecting, no doubt, a reception to which he was accustomed. The commander in chief went loaded down with 750 pounds of silver (worth approximately $36,000 on the current market) and 150 pounds of gold (worth approximately $720,000 on the current market), not to mention ten sets of clothing. But instead of a royal reception, Elisha sent a messenger with the command that he was to "go, wash [himself] seven times in the Jordan" (v. 10).

Naaman was humiliated, both by the poor etiquette and by the poor taste in requiring a man of his station to go and dip in one of the muddiest rivers in the region—at least much more inferior to the fabled rivers from his own homeland in Syria, the Abana and the Pharpar. Was this what all his effort resulted in? He had traveled some 120 miles into a country he had personally invaded only recently. His risks were high. It had all come down to this: the muddy Jordan. It all seemed to be a joke.

Naaman was infuriated that one who was so obviously inferior to himself in social and racial status should have failed to receive him in a proper way. Any prophets he had known in Syria would never have acted that way. They would have been only too glad to have had such an important dignitary visit their residence. His pride was deeply wounded and he was on the brink of abandoning the whole project.

Naaman's servants, with simple, but irrefutable logic, argued, "My father, if the prophet had told you to do some great thing, would you not have done it? How much more, then, when he tells you, 'Wash and be cleansed!'" (v. 13). Just as God had quietly been at work in the proud, egotistical Gentile's life in the victories he had granted to Syria (v. 1), now he was at work in the simple logic of Naaman's own aides.

So instead of returning immediately to Syria, Naaman must go out of his way by heading east to the Jordan River. As this retinue travels from Samaria to the Jordan River, Naaman has time to cool off. It also gives him time to think, for if he is indeed healed, the miracle has little to do with the prophet himself, who by then has distanced himself too far from the scene to get the credit. So to whom does he give the credit? It could not be in the special properties of the waters of the Jordan, for had that been true, why would there be any lepers left in Israel? The answer had to lie elsewhere.

This "great man," who was "highly regarded," a hero and a commander of the Syrian army, went down to the Jordan and began to dip, not once, but seven times. With each dip, he must have become even more dubious of the effectiveness and the validity of such an outrageous demand of so high a ranking man. But, lo and behold, after he had dipped seven times, as the man of God had instructed him, "his flesh was restored and became clean like that of a young boy" (v. 14b).

His first instinct was to head west to Samaria to the home of the prophet Elisha. This time the prophet came out to meet him. As this mighty man stood with his attendants before the prophet Elisha, he confessed, "Now I know that there is no God in all the world except in Israel" (v. 15b). As Walter Maier III noted:

> The gods of Syria, supposedly superior to Yahweh, could not heal Naaman; thus he sees that what he has been taught, and what he has believed about these gods, is false. They are false gods, they are not really gods at all. They are in fact non-existent, and, if such is the case for Syria's gods, that certainly holds for the gods of other nations. Yahweh cured him; Yahweh exists; indeed Yahweh is the only God in all the earth.[3]

It is clear that Naaman has been thoroughly convinced that his healing was distinctively the work of the Lord God of Israel. It is also clear from verse 17 that he believed in Yahweh. But does this amount to saving faith? Has Naaman merely become a monotheist, or even a henotheist? This is the question that is rarely examined in connection with this passage, except for the article previously noted by Maier.

A belief in one God, admirable as that may be, is still not saving faith. The New Testament makes the point in Acts 4:12 that "salvation is found in no one else, for there is no other name under heaven given to men by which we must be saved." Likewise, John 17:3 agrees that a belief in God is not enough: "Now this is eternal life: that they may know you, the only true God and Jesus Christ, whom you have sent."

Some may want to argue that saving faith was different in the Old Testament, but that would go against the plain teaching of the text.[4] All, of course, will agree that salvation in the Old Testament was by grace and faith alone. Most will also agree that when Abraham believed, and as recorded in Genesis 15:6, he was also justified. The difference begins to appear when we ask if the object of faith is the same in the Old Testament as it is in the New. Must Naaman believe in the coming Man of Promise, the "Seed" of the woman and of Abraham and David? And the answer is "Yes." Even in Genesis 15:6, Abraham did more than merely become a monotheist; he believed and put his faith in the promise God had just finished giving (Gen. 15:1–5) about the

3. Ibid., p. 183.
4. See Walter C. Kaiser, Jr., "The Old Testament as the Plan of Salvation," in *Toward Rediscovering the Old Testament* (Grand Rapids: Zondervan, 1987), pp. 121–44. Idem, "Salvation in the Old Testament: With Special Emphasis on the Object and Content of Personal Belief," *Jian Dao: A Journal of Bible and Theology* 2 (1994): 1–18.

"Seed" that would come through the line established by God. Faith terminated and was grounded in the Messiah who was to come. Thus, both the method and object of saving faith in both Testaments was the same.

But did enough evidence about the coming Messiah exist at this time? Our answer again is that there was adequate information. This word could be traced from Genesis 3:15, with its promise about that coming male descendant from the seed of Eve to the line of Shem (Gen. 9:27), where God would come and take up his dwelling. It continued in the oft-repeated promise given to the patriarchs that in that Seed all the families of the earth would be blessed. That blessing would come through Judah, the fourth son of Jacob (Gen. 49:8–10), who would rise as a star out of Jacob (Num. 24). This Coming One would be a "prophet" (Deut. 18:15ff.), "priest" (Ps. 110:4), and "king" (2 Sam. 7:16; Ps. 2:6).

Had General Naaman been told more not only about the prophet in Israel, but also about the promise God had given, a promise that was to all the peoples of the earth? Had the captured maiden witnessed not only about the miracle-working power of Elisha, but about Yahweh whose plan embraced all the families of the earth?

One thing is for sure: Naaman is the first one to mention (2 Kings 5) the name "Yahweh," both before (v. 11), and after (v. 15) his healing. He could just as easily have used the plural noun "Elohim," "God," to refer to the God of Israel. The Old Testament is careful about the times it chooses to refer to Yahweh. That name was reserved for those who had a personal relationship to him, otherwise Elohim was accurate enough.

What strengthens the argument that Naaman had a much greater knowledge of the God of Israel than what the text feels is necessary to describe is that he immediately speaks of making "burnt offerings" to Yahweh (v. 17). What possessed him to make this connection? And why did he feel the need to ask permission, indeed, forgiveness to accompany his king into a pagan temple (v. 18)?

Obviously, this mighty Syrian general had now properly humbled himself, for he refers to himself five times (vv. 15, 17 *bis,* 18 *bis*) as "your servant" when speaking to Elisha. Standing before the prophet, he offers the magnificent gifts he has brought along—gifts that could no doubt be put to good use in the school of the prophets. But Elisha refuses to let Naaman get even a hint of the error that he had in any way paid for either his physical healing or his spiritual redemption.

But what of Naaman's speech in verses 17–18? Is it not most odd? Indeed, this new convert mixes his new Yahwism with strands of an old paganism. There are three requests that he makes of the prophet. (1) He requests permission to take back to Syria two muleloads of Israelite soil so he can be on good grounds when he worships Yahweh. This is nothing more than the pervasive ancient Near Eastern belief that religion was territorial and that each god was effective only on his own territory.[5] (2) He wanted the soil in order to offer up "burnt offerings and sacrifices" to Yahweh when he returned to Syria, again on the basis that Yahweh could only be worshiped on his own ground. Interestingly enough, Naaman had confessed that "There is no God *in* all the earth but *in* Israel" (v. 15), but he has yet to realize that Yahweh is God *of* all the earth, and not just in Israel.[6] (3) He asked to be forgiven by the prophet when he accompanied his king into the temple of Rimmon, the chief god of Syria. Rimmon was also known as Hadad, or Baal, who was the storm and fertility god found in several Semitic cultures of that day.

To each of the three requests, Elisha made no other response than this: "Go in peace" (v. 19a). Whatever could the prophet have meant by that? Was this tacit approval of Naaman's way of thinking? Did the prophet give his approval to each of the three requests since this was in another era, in Old Testament times? Several have argued that way.[7]

It is apparent that Naaman has changed, for his attitude is now one of being Elisha's servant rather than his superior. No longer is he contemptuous of Israel and her dirty River Jordan, but now he wishes to take back some of Israel's soil. But should not Elisha correct his syncretistic ways?

Naaman was uncomfortable with his own requests, thereby showing that his conscience bothered him. He asked, "May Yahweh forgive your servant for this" (v. 18). Therefore, it is doubtful that Elisha was intending to express his approbation when he said rather elliptically, "Go in peace."

Walter A. Maier III surveys a series of possible meanings that the prophet's parting words could have.[8] If he was not indicating his approval of Naaman's way of thinking, could it mean that he was recognizing that Naaman was from a different culture? But that would make culture sovereign over the revelation of God. Could it be a matter of a believer's

---

5. See 1 Kings 20:23 and 2 Kings 17:26 for other texts describing this localized form of religion and the power of the gods.

6. This fine point is another that was made by Maier, "Healing of Naaman," p. 187.

7. Ibid., p. 189, cites several commentators who took this approach to this question. James L. Crenshaw, *Story and Faith: A Guide to the Old Testament* (New York: Macmillan, 1986), pp. 149–50; Gwilym H. Jones, *First and Second Kings,* 2 vols., New Century Bible Commentary (Grand Rapids: Eerdmans, 1984), 2:419.

8. Maier, "Healing of Naaman," pp. 188–94.

sphere of liberty? Hardly, for the issue Naaman raised was not in the category of minor issues versus essential doctrines of the faith. The man's own conscience would not allow him to do some of these things—consequently, he asked for forgiveness.

Maier is correct when he concludes that Elisha expressed in his salutation his confidence that the God who had brought this Gentile to faith, through however fragmentary or fulsome the testimony of the Israelite maiden, was able to bring this Gentile to spiritual growth. Maier continues:

> In verse 19a the prophet says "go in peace" because he wants the flame of faith which has started in Naaman to continue burning and not be snuffed out. The flame in the new convert is still small; Elisha does not want to quench what has just begun in Naaman with a strong negative response or with instruction which, too hastily given, only would confuse and upset. He handles Naaman tenderly, as a spiritual babe. The prophet realizes that if at this moment he is too critical and makes too many demands Naaman will feel discouraged, weighted down, and "turned off" to Yahwehism. Some of the Syrian's old pagan notions still cling to him, and he is not ready to give up his high position. . . .Therefore the prophet makes no comment about the soil, the sacrifices, the bowing down to Rimmon, or, for that matter, the importance of circumcision, and attending the annual feasts in Jerusalem.[9]

Conclusion

Yahweh was the Lord of all the nations even during Old Testament times. Not only had he used a pagan Gentile general to carry out the battles with the results he had wanted, but he was also using the witness of a little girl who, having been put into most trying of circumstances, was used as a forerunner of the diaspora that would spread the Good News of the promise-plan of God.

It is clear that God's mission was not exclusively Jewish in the Old Testament. While Israel remains at the center of the story, this is not to say that there was not a globalization of the gospel in view. Nor is it possible to argue that the maiden's witness was only passive, rather than active, in form. Had that little maiden not spoken up so forthrightly and confi-

9. Ibid., p. 193. Of course, not everything is told us about the faith of Melchizedek, Jethro, Rahab, Ruth, or Naaman. Our argument is that they all put their trust in the same Christ mentioned in the New Testament under the Old Testament terms of "seed," Man of Promise, "Star," "Rock," or the like.

dently, Naaman would have remained in more trouble than his skin condition. He had to have his sin condition cared for as well.

Why spend so much space in the biblical narrative to tell this story? Should one claim that it was to magnify the miracle-working power of the prophet, then why did the text not focus more on that one aspect? And why was the prophet not carried directly to the scene of the Jordan so that a tie-in could be made?

Only one explanation will satisfy all the data: the divine revelation wanted us to see that Yahweh was truly calling all the families of the earth—even one's enemies—to the same Savior and salvation. Nothing could force God to bestow his gifts of grace or mercy, not even those of royalty or position. But then, neither could ethnicity detract from his plan to spread his grace far and wide.

In fact, as a result of Naaman's dramatic healing and conversion, the prophet Elisha made a visit to Damascus (2 Kings 8:7–15) late in the reign of Jehoram. It was then that Ben-Hadad II heard of his presence in the capital of Syria. He sent his servant Hazael to Elisha to learn whether he, too, would recover from his sickness. The messenger learned that he himself would be the next to usurp the throne, which he promptly carried out.

Notice, however, the range of the prophet's activity, which was not unusual, given the way many other Old Testament prophets both made personal appearances in foreign nations and used diplomatic channels to communicate messages from Yahweh to these pagans. It is not too much of a jump in logic to assume that just as Jonah was a preacher of righteousness in the capital of Nineveh, so Elisha and the company of the prophets likewise delivered the message of the saving grace of God to Syria as well. In fact, Jesus cites this same line of thought in his Nazareth sermon in Luke 4.

FOUR

God's Call to Israel to Be a Light to the Nations

IN THE polytheistic way of thinking, one's god was linked to the people and their homeland, but in the revelatory scheme of things, Scripture refused to put Yahweh in such a straitjacket. Yahweh was always the only one, true God who ruled over all creation and all nations and all peoples.

True, one could, for the sake of argument, point to Judges 11:24 as a contradictory argument, and claim that the Old Testament taught that other gods were sovereign over their own territories. In this passage, the biblical judge Jephthah in his dispute with the Ammonites said, "Will you not take what your god Chemosh gives you? Likewise, whatever the LORD our God has given us, we will possess." But one should not take this to be a normative statement but rather a report of how this rough-and-ready judge responded to those who claimed that the territory in question was theirs. Jephthah's point was if that was the case, then why had no one thought to take it back in the past three hundred years? (Judg. 11:25–26). The issue of why the Ammonites had failed to take back the territory they claimed as their own was so overwhelming that comment on points of theology about any gods of these lands seemed unnecessary at the moment.

A similar argument is often mounted from 1 Kings 20:23, where the officials of the king of Syria were attempting to rationalize their military losses to the king. They opined, "Their gods are the gods of the hills. That is why they were too strong for us." But, once again, orthodox theology cannot be built from the opinions of heathen. Their statement may even indicate that this was what many thought in that day, but it would be an unwarranted leap in logic to conclude that therefore this is what Scripture taught prior to the days of the prophet Isaiah and his so-called "new" universalism.

Since this was part of the populist thought of the day, the prophet Isaiah anticipated the complaint that the coming Babylonian exile would be regarded as the defeat of Yahweh. But that view would be misguided, taught Isaiah, for the defeat of Judah by Babylon and the subsequent exile of the nation was an expression of Yahweh's judgment on a renegade people who refused to obey their God. Isaiah thundered:

> Who handed Jacob over to become loot,
> And Israel to the plunderers?
> Was it not the LORD,
> Against whom we have sinned?
> For they would not follow his ways;
> They did not obey his law.
> So he poured out on them his burning anger,
> The violence of war.
> It enveloped them in flames,
> Yet they did not understand;
> It consumed them,
> But they did not take it to heart. (Isa. 42:24–25)

This, however, was not enough. Simply to explain why the nation would suffer such a devastating defeat did not go far enough in vindicating the sovereignty and majesty of Yahweh before all the other nations, much less one's own people. The gods of the nations and their peoples had to face up to the fact that Israel's God should be their God as well.

Accordingly, Isaiah depicts a court scene right in the beginning of that famous section of Isaiah 40–55. In Isaiah 41:21–29 the messenger of God speaks on God's behalf and demands that the idol-gods of the Gentile nations "present [their] case" and "set forth [their] strong arguments." Three tests are posed for these alleged deities to pass:

1. Can any of these idol-gods interpret past history in such a way as to bring to light history's underlying purpose?

2. Can they forecast or show anything that is going to happen in the future and thereby demonstrate that they are real gods?
3. Can they do anything, good or bad, in the course of events so we can know they are alive and real?[1]

All of these challenges were calls for the idol-gods to give some evidence and proof that they were real and that they could effect changes in the course of human history. Alas, not a word, not a peep, not an answer was heard from these fakes.

Isaiah 46–48 contains a trilogy of chapters that announce judgment of the gods of Babylon. Bel, or, Marduk, as he was also known, the titular deity of Babylon, along with Nebo (as in the name King Nabopolassar), the titular deity of the Babylonian royal family, are depicted as being hauled away on carts to escape the coming conquest of King Cyrus of Medo-Persia. Alas, however, the cart overturns and the gods fall out. It is almost as if the prophet sneers with, "Hey, is that the best you gods can do? Can't you even save yourselves? If so, your worshipers have very little chance of escaping from the debacle that is coming upon Babylon."

All through this section of Isaiah 40–48 the prophet taunts these gods for how worthless they are in comparison to the Living God. The ridiculousness of depending on those who cannot speak, see, or do anything is mind-boggling. Isaiah 44:9–19 calls for those who make these "nothings" to think for a moment: half of the wood you use for fuel and the other half for the image. The thing is blind and ignorant, and can profit its worshipers nothing.

But over against that is the challenge of the One to whom there is no comparison (Isa. 44:7). If only the Gentiles would come to their senses and realize that the God of Israel is not a national God, but the Lord of all the earth. He alone is God of all the nations!

But it was precisely at this point that Isaiah triumphantly declared that Yahweh rose to the same challenge and provided these very proofs of his sovereignty over all nations and peoples. The parade example that the prophet points to, on behalf of Yahweh, is the fact that he will raise up Cyrus, the Medo-Persian king (Isa. 41:25, 26; 45:1). Cyrus's appearance, along with Babylon's stunning victory, are all being announced *in advance* precisely so that when the unlikely events take place, it will be clearly recog-

---

1. Walter C. Kaiser, Jr., *Back Toward the Future: Hints for Interpreting Biblical Prophecy* (Grand Rapids: Baker, 1989), pp. 17–27.

nized that Yahweh is the only true God and that he has power and control over all humanity and all history.

Compared to Yahweh, the nations were but a drop in the bucket (Isa. 40:15, 17) and the inhabitants of the universe were by comparison, again, "grasshoppers" (Isa. 40:22). Therefore, the question was simply this: "To whom, then, will you compare God? What image will you compare him to?" "Who is my equal? says the Holy One" (Isa. 40:18). Clearly, no volunteers stepped forward and the question had an implied obvious answer of "No one!"

Now if Yahweh was the only true God and all the idol-gods were "nothings," there ought to be some corollaries to these conclusions. But Isaiah will first heap scathing scorn and sarcasm on the idol-gods. In chapter 46 he depicted these Babylonian images being carted around like so much baggage that needed to be cared for. Yet Yahweh was not carried by anyone; instead, he carried his people rather than burdening them with the job of carrying him around.

Indeed, Israel herself was a standing witness to the power and reality of who Yahweh was and what he had done in their history. "You are my witnesses," Yahweh affirmed in that classic passage that contrasted the nonexistent idol-god witness and the summons for the nation of Israel to rise to the occasion (Isa. 43:10–13).

It is this theme of the nation Israel as witness that introduces our subject of mission in the Old Testament prophets. This is seen particularly in the Servant of the Lord poems, principally Isaiah 42:1, 6 and 49:6.

> Here is my servant, whom I uphold,
>   My chosen one in whom I delight;
> I have put my Spirit on him
>   And he will bring justice to the nations. (Isa. 42:1)

> I, the LORD [Yahweh], have called you in righteousness;
> I will take hold of your hand.
> I will keep you
>   and will make you to be a covenant for the peoples
>   And a light for the Gentiles. (Isa. 42:6)

> It is too small a thing for you to be my servant
> to restore the tribes of Jacob
> and bring back those of Israel I have kept.
> I will also make you a light for the Gentiles,
> That you may bring my salvation to the ends of
> The earth. (Isa. 49:6)

All of this raises questions: Who is the "Servant"? What was the "justice" or "judgment" that this Servant was to bring? Was it some sort of political exercise of some kind of government over the nations? Or, should the word "justice" be rendered "manner" or "ordinance," meaning that the Servant would introduce the practice of religion among the nations?

One thing was for sure: Yahweh would restore his people Israel from all over the world "so that from the rising of the sun to the place of its setting all might know there is none besides [Yahweh]" (Isa. 45:6). Accordingly, all would see that "the Holy One of Israel is your Redeemer, he is called the God of all the earth" (Isa. 54:5).

Isaiah's Universalism

It was much more common at the beginning of the twentieth century for scholars to argue that Isaiah's message was one of centrifugal universalism. They interpreted the prophet as affirming that Yahweh was the only God and that all nations must come to know him. But even more affirming was the fact that they argued that it was Israel's duty to make God's name known to the ends of the earth.[2] However, disappointingly, many of these same interpreters also argued that from the time of the exodus until the time of the writing of Isaiah 40–55 (which many incorrectly attributed to a Deutero-Isaiah, who came after the exile in the fifth century), Israel's missionary duty was only centripetal and not centrifugal.

More recently, however, Bernard Wodecki demonstrated that the case for worldwide missions could be found throughout the entire Book of Isaiah.[3] Wodecki identified the Servant of the Lord with the Messiah, whom he believed Isaiah taught, will bring the Law and teaching of Yahweh to the ends of the earth through the witness of his people Israel.

---

2. For example, H. H. Rowley, *The Missionary Message of the Old Testament* (London: Carey Kingsgate, 1944), p. 50, could cite Isa. 45:21ff. as one of several texts that supported this duty for the nation of Israel to reach out as a witness. This reference was called to my attention by Michael A. Grisanti, "Israel's Mission to the Nations in Isaiah 40–55: An Update," *The Master's Seminary Journal* 9 (1998): 46, n. 21.

3. As pointed out by Grisanti, "Israel's Mission," p. 48, n. 30. Bernard Wodecki, "Heilsuniversalismus im Buck des Propheten Jesaja," in *Dein Wort Bedachten: Alttestamentliche Aufsatze*, ed. J. Reindl and G. Henschel (Leipzig: St. Benno-Verlag, 1981), pp. 76– 101. Wodecki's work reflects his 1977 doctoral dissertation, which dealt with universal salvation in the first part of Isaiah, "Der Heilsuniversalismus beim Propheten Proto-Jesaja" [the German title of the Polish dissertation; English, "Universal Salvation According to the Prophet Proto-Isaiah"] (Ph.D. diss., University of Warsaw, 1977). Wodecki wrote on p. 99 that "the Spirit of universal salvation permeates the entire book of Isaiah."

More recently scholarship, sadly enough, has shifted and views Israel's role in bringing the message of salvation to the Gentiles only by means of mediation, but not by active witnessing. This made Israel's witness merely a passive one. But this opinion must be tested against the evidence found in the Servant Songs of Isaiah.

The Servant of the Lord

If any credence is given to an active role for the sending out of the message of the gospel, it is credited to Messiah's role as found in the Servant Songs as opposed to the nationalism found in the rest of the Book of Isaiah. In that case, which we will go on to deny here, the Servant figure of the Messiah replaces Israel as the active dispenser of the word of God to the nations and to the ends of the earth.

Accordingly, scholarship is divided at the moment between those who believe that Isaiah teaches that Israel offers no salvation for the Gentiles and those who believe that Isaiah picks up the informing and antecedent theology of the Abrahamic promise and the message of Exodus 19:4–6 to remind the nation of her duty to be a witness (both actively or passively) to the pagan people groups around the world.

The solution to this debate, it would seem, is first of all to identify the "Servant of the Lord," and then to learn what his tasks and mission are.

It is noteworthy that the term "servant" is found twenty times exclusively in the singular form in Isaiah 40–53, and eleven times exclusively in the plural form in Isaiah 54–66.[4] In order to show how the singular and plural could both work here, our conclusion is that the "Servant of the Lord" is a corporate term that embodies at one and the same time a reference to the One, who is the representative of the whole, and the whole group that belongs to that single whole.

To demonstrate that the single idea of this corporate figure represents a collective term that points to an individual as well as to the whole group that the individual represents, let us examine how it is used by the prophet.

- The Servant is the whole nation of Israel in twelve out of the twenty references (41:8–10; 43:8–13; 43:14–44:5; 44:6–8, 21–23; 44:24–45:13; 48:1, 7, 10–12, 17).

4. The plural forms for "servants" are located in Isa. 54:17; 56:6; 63:17; 65:8–9, 13 *(ter)*, 14–15; 66:14.

- The four great Servant Songs of Isaiah all present the servant as an individual who ministers to Israel (42:1–7; 49:1–6; 50:4–9; 52:13–53:12). To reject the corporate solidarity of the Servant figure is to leave oneself with an unsoluable enigma in these songs, or at least a flat contradiction in divine revelation.

The fact that the "Servant of the Lord" is a collective and corporate term is no more unexpected at this stage in the divine revelation than is the fact the "seed of Abraham" is likewise a similar type of term. It, too, embraced the One who represented the whole group by the singular collective word "seed." As a matter of fact, Israel is called the "servant" who is the "seed of Abraham" in Isaiah 41:8. Moreover, Moses had used the term "servant" of Abraham, Isaac, and Jacob already in Exodus 32:13 and Deuteronomy 9:27. All Israel was regarded as God's "servants" in Leviticus 25:42, 55. As John Bright put it:

> The figure of the Servant oscillates between the individual and the group. . . . He is the coming Redeemer of the true Israel who in his suffering makes the fulfillment of Israel's task possible; he is the central actor in the "new thing" that is about to take place.[5]

As further evidence that this corporate thesis is the correct one, it is interesting to note that in the four Servant Songs mentioned above, many of the individual's title or descriptions are matched by an identical ascription made of Israel elsewhere in the Book of Isaiah. For example:

Used of an Individual	The Title or Function	Used of All Israel
42:1	"My chosen"	41:8–9
49:3	"My servant"	44:21
49:6	"a light to the nations"	42:6; 51:4
49:1	"called me from womb"	44:2, 24; 43:1
4:1	"named by name"	43:1b

Despite the striking nature of this evidence, the Servant of the songs has as his task and mission the work "to bring Israel back" and "to gather" the nation to himself (Isa. 49:5–6). That is what makes it impossible to totally equate the Servant with Israel in all respects. But this is not surprising, for we have seen the same oscillation in the collective terms used

5. John Bright, *Kingdom of God* (Nashville: Abingdon, 1953), p. 159f.

earlier of the Man of Promise who was to come and of those who believed in him.

The Servant of the Lord, then, is the messianic person in the Abrahamic, Davidic line that finally eventuates in the new David, who is also known as the Seed, God's Holy One *(Ḥāsîd),* the Branch, and so on. But, the Servant is no less the nation Israel that participates in that collective whole.

So what about this Servant being a "light to the nations/Gentiles" (Isa. 42:6; 49:6)? The nation of Israel, as "servant," is called to be that light to the nations. This is practically a replication of the promise made through Abraham that "in you shall all the families of the earth be blessed" (Gen. 12:3).

The people of Israel were to exemplify their calling to be a kingdom of priests in their service to the Gentiles. It is this theme that the Servant Songs take up. This affirmation came to a climax in the Servant's role to be "a light to the Gentiles, that you may bring my salvation to the ends of the earth" (Isa. 42:6). There can be little question that the mission was a spiritual one, not a political one.

But to come to the question more directly, we must ask whether the nation Israel was sent to be Yahweh's witness. The answer can be found in Isaiah 42:1, 4, 6.

> Here is my servant, whom I uphold,
> My chosen one in whom I delight;
> I will put my Spirit on him
> And he will bring justice to the nations.
>
> . . . he will not falter or be discouraged
> till he establishes justice on earth.
> In his law the nations will put their hope.
>
> "I, the LORD [Yahweh] , have called you in righteousness;
> I will take hold of your hand.
> I will keep you and make you to be a covenant for the people
> And a light for the Gentiles."

Three expressions are critical in determining Israel's role in missions in the Old Testament: (1) What is the meaning of "justice" in verses 1 and 4? (2) What is the "covenant for the people" in verse 6? (3) What does it mean to be "a light to the Gentiles" and who is to be that light? These expressions must now be studied one at a time.

The Meaning of "Justice"

The basic meaning of the Hebrew word *mišpāṭ* is judicial. All concede this point. But what is not clear is whether contextually this "justice" or "judgment" is a positive or a negative concept here. Does it have a political promise to the effect, that the Servant will set up some kind of government over the nations, or is it to be translated as "manner" as it is in 2 Kings 17:26? There *mišpāṭ* occurs twice in the clause that " the people . . . do not know the 'manner' of the gods of the country." Again in Jeremiah 5:4 the same Hebrew word appears in parallelism with "the way of the LORD": "the 'ordinance/requirements' of their God."[6] If this translation is adopted, then the meaning is that the Servant's role was to establish the practice or manner of serving Yahweh among the nations. This conclusion would be more in keeping with the climax of the Servant Song, where the Servant's mission is to restore Israel and to be a light to the Gentiles.

The debate over the proper translation of this word *mišpāṭ* is enormous, with few in agreement. But only the missionary interpretation seems to solve all the exegetical considerations in the best way. *Mišpāṭ* is "instruction in judgment or the right." This is affirmed also by the parallel word *tôrâ* ("instruction in the right way") in verse 4—"In his law [*tôrâ*] the islands [= distant countries] will put their hope." This interpretation of *mišpāṭ* as religion comes, then, from the context. The idea of mission is further enhanced by the fact that the nations must "wait" for this law. This waiting is one with expectancy.

Isaiah 42:1 also indicates that an endowment of the Spirit would be necessary if the Servant were to accomplish his task. It would seem then that the task is a spiritual one and not a judicial or political one as de Boer[7] and Beuken[8] strongly argued.

Isaiah 42:1–4 makes a statement that the Servant, here understood as the whole believing group of Israel, with their representative of the whole group, will engage in active mission work on behalf of all the nations. In this role as a missionary servant, they would bring true religion, the right way and the "manner," for the nations to follow.

6. A. Gelston, "The Missionary Message of Second Isaiah," *Scottish Journal of Theology* 18 (1965): 315.

7. P. A. H. de Boer, *Second Isaiah's Message*, p. 91, who was followed by Martin-Achard, *Light to the Nations*, p. 26, n. 11.

8. W. A. M. Beuken, "*Mishpat:* The First Servant Song in its Context," *Vetus Testamentum* 22 (1972): 6.

The Covenant for the People

The Hebrew expression *librît 'am*, "to be a covenant for the people," is the key phrase in this whole study of the Servant's missionary role.

Some will immediately object to equating the word "people" with the nations. True, the word does occur in the singular form and not the plural, but it is incorrect to state, as Snaith[9] does, that the word for "people" means only "Israel" when it is in the singular in Isaiah 40–66, while the plural form is reserved for the nations. This is an overstatement, for there are clear exceptions (Isa. 40:7; 42:5), where the singular refers to the nations in both cases.

Note also the close proximity of the "people" and the "nations": "a covenant for the people and a light for the nations/Gentiles." Add to this the universal reference in verse 5 ("and gives life to those who walk on [the earth]"). That is why "to be a covenant for the people" must be taken to mean that all the Gentiles and nations of the earth are to be consolidated in the same covenant that Yahweh has made with Israel. This covenant sharing with the Gentiles comes from Israel's joining the Messiah in being "a light to the nations."

The reference to "a covenant for the people" demonstrates that the servant cannot be simply identified with all Israel, but with a faithful remnant within that group. The "people" (Hebrew: *'am*) implies some kind of existing relationship between themselves and God. This "covenant" may be the New Covenant with the blessings spelled out in Jeremiah 31:31–34. As such, it would only confirm the Abrahamic covenant, for it too spoke of the blessing for the nations (Gen. 12:3 *et al.*).

The Light for the Gentiles

This phrase occurs twice, in Isaiah 42:6 and 49:6, and is important to the case for missions in the Old Testament. The attempt to avoid the natural meaning of this phrase has produced some ingenious exegesis. Martin-Achard's position is the most telling of all. He deleted this phrase from Isaiah 42:6 because it was not in the Septuagint manuscripts. Therefore, he concluded that it was an interpolation from Isaiah 49:6. But stronger

9. Norman H. Snaith, " Isaiah 40–66. A Study of the Teaching of the Second Isaiah and its Consequences," *Studies in the Second Part of the Book of Isaiah: Supplements to Vetus Testamentum* 14 (1967): 157. Snaith recognized that this was an overstatement, but he regarded "surely the people is grass" in 40:7 as "as clear a case of a gloss as one could find." Snaith must delete evidence fatal to his position.

support than this is needed for the deletion of this phrase.[10] It does occur, as a matter of fact, both in Isaiah 42:6 and 49:6 in all of the best Hebrew manuscripts.

"The light for the Gentiles" is also assigned as a specific mission for the Servant. If we are correct in seeing that the Servant is a corporate term here, then it is clear that Israel is being addressed and encouraged by the Lord to be that witness to the Gentiles. Yahweh will take hold of that remnant of Israel by the hand to guide them in this work of witnessing, just as certainly as he called them in righteousness. Is this not why the apostle Paul in Acts 13:47 could take this very same text and declare, "This is what the Lord has commanded *us* [Paul and Barnabas]: 'I have made you a light for the Gentiles, that you may bring salvation to the ends of the earth.'" Later in his career, Paul stood on trial for his life before King Agrippa in Acts 26:22 and affirmed: "I am saying nothing beyond what the prophets and Moses said would happen." He did not see himself as an innovator, or as one who introduced meanings that were not already in the text. Therefore, it is hard to see his application of the words of Isaiah 42:6 and 49:6 to himself and to Barnabas as being out of line with the plain assertion of the original Old Testament meaning. These New Testament believers saw Isaiah 49:6 to be an authorization addressed directly to them, just as surely as the audience of Isaiah's day understood it.

Of course, Simeon did take the baby Jesus in his arms (Luke 2:32) and declare that the baby, too, was "a light for revelation to the Gentiles." But that is because of the corporate nature of the Servant figure, who simultaneously represents the One and the many.

We conclude, therefore, that salvation was to come to the Gentiles through the mediation of Yahweh's Servant Messiah and Israel. It has become fashionable to limit the fulfillment of this role of Israel to times yet future to our own day. But when our Lord gave his promise of the Holy Spirit, and his plan in Acts 1:8 that the early Christian believers were to be his witnesses in Jerusalem, Judea, and Samaria and to the ends of the earth, he authoritatively gave the meaning of what he had intended for the listeners of Isaiah's day to understand from Isaiah 49:6.

There are three repeated allusions to this text from the prophet in the New Testament. (1) The expression "to the ends of the earth" is verbally identical to the Greek rendering of the same phrase in Isaiah 49:6. The extent and scope of the witness are the same in both Testaments.

---

10. Martin-Achard, *Light to the Nations*, p. 27.

(2) The coming of the Holy Spirit in Acts 1:8 is closest to the wording in Isaiah 32:15, where the destruction of Jerusalem is predicted "till the Spirit is poured upon us from on high, and the desert becomes a fertile field." This is reminiscent of the Spirit's coming in Isaiah 44:3–4 as rain on a dry and thirsty land. In this context, the clause, "I will pour out my Spirit on your offspring, and my blessing on your descendants" (Isa. 44:3b) does not refer to abundant rain, but is used metaphorically of the conferring of spiritual blessings. Thus, as numerous progeny was taken as a sign of God's blessing, so spiritual progeny are likewise a sign of God's blessing. The work of the Holy Spirit would elicit bold testimony from his people Israel, just as it will from early Christian believers.

(3) The Lord summons his servant Israel to be his witnesses. What makes this necessary contextually is that this summons is given to Israel in the context of Yahweh's lawsuit against the idols that the pagans served (Isa. 41:1–4; 43:8–12; 44:8). The idol-gods had been challenged to present their case and to bring forth as many witnesses as they needed to prove their claim. But these witnesses are blind (Isa. 44:9, 18–20), and without life and unable to answer calls for deliverance (Isa. 44:17). Over against these witnesses, the Lord subpoenas Israel to be his witnesses, for Israel had seen his miraculous redemption in their history (Isa. 43:10, 12). True, the Lord's Servant-messenger, Israel, is also blind, not because she trusted in idols like the Gentiles, but because they did not trust God to do all he had promised (Isa. 42:18–19). Yet God promised to heal the blind eyes of his Servant Israel and "make them a covenant for the people and a light for the Gentiles" (Isa. 49:6).

In the inaugurated eschatology taught in Scripture, the biblical text has both a "now" and a "not yet" aspect to it. This is true of Isaiah 49:22–26, where Yahweh promises his Servant-messenger that he "will beckon to the Gentiles" until "all mankind will know that I the LORD, am your Savior, your redeemer, the Mighty One of Jacob." Even kings and queens will "bow down" and "lick the dust of your feet," an obvious allusion to Genesis 3:14. In this latter text, what is said of the "Serpent," the Devil, can be applied by corporate solidarity to all unbelievers, who will likewise bite the dust so that they might come to the end of themselves and desire to know the Lord God and how he can redeem them regardless of their ethnic background.

Conclusion

The prophet Isaiah surely called his nation to function actively as a missionary to the Gentiles and nations at large. The case for an active mis-

sionary call to Israel is exceedingly strong in the two Servant Song:
Isaiah 42 and 49.

Once it is admitted that Israel also functioned and was designated as
"Servant of the Lord," it is difficult to limit her involvement in the spre
of the gospel simply to a passive role of centripetally calling the nations
the world to herself. She must bring the religious teaching, usually tran
lated "bring justice," to the nations. The instruction as to what is right mu:
come from those who have been entrusted with the oracles of God.

But she was marked out long ago in the time of Abraham "to be a
covenant to the people" of the earth. Once the word "people" is shown to
be equal to the Gentile nations of the earth, then it must mean that all the
Gentiles and peoples of the world are to be consolidated in the very same
covenant that Yahweh had made with Abraham, Isaac, Jacob, and David
and that Jeremiah spelled out in the New Covenant. All these covenants
had the same basic core even though new features were added. But the
peoples that were included in the blessings of these covenants were the
same. They were initially given to Israel so that Israel could share them
with all the peoples of the earth.

What really puts the final clincher on this argument is that the task of
being "the light to the Gentiles" is assigned to the Servant. In this role,
Yahweh will take the hand of the remnant of Israel and guide them in the
work of witnessing. If any doubts still remain, then notice how the apostle Paul takes this identical word given to this Servant and declares in Acts
13:47 that this is the same word that explains why he, too, went to the
Gentiles. The command, then, was not limited to the Messiah as Servant,
but it also embraced the remnant of Israel.

If any doubts remain as to how far Israel was to go with this message,
that too is abundantly clear in this text of Isaiah: it was "to the ends of the
earth."

Such a witness must not be carried out on Israel's own power, but the
Holy Spirit would come on this remnant like rain on a dry and thirsty land.
So Israel must witness on behalf of the Lord, just as the pagans were to
call on their idol-gods to speak up and demonstrate that they were indeed
deities. All their speaking up as servant-messengers must reach out to
beckon the Gentiles until all humanity has had a chance to know that the
Lord is the only Savior, Redeemer, and Mighty One over all.

FIVE

God's Persuasion of Jonah to Be His Witness with Other Prophets from Israel

THE BOOK of Jonah is the account of a man who was sent by God to preach in the capital city of Assyria, Nineveh. But instead of obeying this divine call to go warn this nation that it had only forty days in which to repent and get right with Yahweh, the God of all the earth, Jonah tried to escape this mission. But he was no more successful in escaping his call than was the prophet Jeremiah.

When Jonah sought to flee from God and the mission assigned to him, the hand of God pursued him and finally brought him, after some harrowing experiences, to Nineveh. There, he finally preached his message of judgment that had such an effect on the whole city, from top to bottom, that the king and people put on sackcloth as a sign of their contrition and repentance. Thus the threatened judgment was averted in the nick of time.

It was the prophet who did not fare too well. He was deeply disappointed that these Assyrians, the most barbaric of enemies that the nation of Israel had faced up to that point, should have escaped a destruction that was so close at hand. Thus, the book ends with Nineveh having been spared, but the messenger Jonah bitter, surly, and despondent over the mercy and graciousness of God.

The Critical Estimate of the Book of Jonah

The almost universal conclusion of critical scholarship is that the story of Jonah is not a historical happening. Given this assumption, it is not surprising that this has led many to reject Jonah as a missionary book. For example, Harry Orlinsky declared that since, in his estimation, Jonah was a postexilic fictional work, no example of an Israelite prophet to the nations could be adduced.[1]

However, both the critical estimate of the literary genre and the dating of the Book of Jonah are incorrect. Therefore the conclusion that Jonah has no relevance to the question of mission in the Old Testament is suspect because the assumptions are unconfirmed.

With the exception of Jonah 2:2–9, the book is a straightforward narrative, even though it is somewhat unusual due to its lack of background material and historical detail. This detail was probably omitted in order not to weaken the main impact of the story. Interestingly, it was only after the nineteenth century that Jonah was no longer regarded as history. A few skeptics prior to that time had choked on the miracles in the book, but the first outright denial that it was historical came from J. G. Eichhorn in 1823.

To argue, as has been done frequently, that the book is either an allegory, satire, or parable is to raise the issue of the proper criteria for each of these literary types. G. Ch. Aalders[2] pressed the quest for such criteria based on other literary examples of each alleged type. With allegory and parable, the story was too long and the details too complex to produce any consistency among interpreters as to the meaning of the allegory or parable. As for satire, except for short clauses or phrases, there were no *extended* examples in the biblical corpus of this genre being used. Even Philo (first century A.D.), who was the best-known sponsor of the allegorical interpretation of biblical texts, was very explicit that the fish and story of Jonah be taken naturally or literally.

Nor did the late dating fare any better. To allege that the story was written in the time of Ezra and Nehemiah as a protest against narrow-minded nationalism and exclusivism, its effectiveness would rest almost entirely

---

1. Harry M. Orlinsky, "Nationalism—Universalism in the Book of Jeremiah," in *Essays in Biblical Culture and Bible Translation* (New York: Ktav, 1974), p. 133.
2. G. Ch. Aalders, *The Problem of the Book of Jonah* (London: Tyndale House, 1948).

on its being received as the truth by its audience. The argument for taking the postexilic date is the reference to the past tense in Jonah 3:3 ("Now Nineveh *was* an important city") and the difference in style between the eighth-century prophet Hosea and Jonah. Especially telling, it was thought, were the number of Aramaisms in the Book of Jonah.

But the verb "was" cannot be read to mean that the city had been overthrown long before the events narrated in the book imply. It may mean no more than the fact that this was the state of affairs now at the time of writing. The Hebrew form of the verb could just as easily have been translated: "Now Nineveh had [already] become a great city." As for the question of the difference in style, it cannot be proven that there was a distinctive style that belonged to the northern prophets of the eighth century B.C. The same criticism could also be made for the list of Aramaisms. There is a growing list of words in Aramaic that at one time were thought to be late, but which now are turning up in earlier documents. Therefore, the use of Aramaic words is not a dependable criterion for assigning lateness to a passage or a book.

Jesus also referred to Jonah as a historical personage (Matt. 12:38–41; Luke 11:29–30, 32). It is difficult to argue that Jesus could not distinguish among allegory, parable, and history. So strong is this argument that some have decided the best way to handle this objection is to deny that Jesus mentioned Jonah at all. To say that our Lord merely accommodated his views to those arguments that he knew were current among the people to whom he spoke is to make a hard case for Jesus selectively going along with the culture at one time and directly opposing it at other times. Why did Jesus not take the same tack when it came to the question of the Temple, for the Jews heard him attacking their traditions on that question?

Scholarly Opinion on Jonah as a Missionary Book

Earlier in the twentieth century, many scholars favored viewing Jonah as a book of missionary activity. One could cite the works of James D. Smart, R. K. Harrison, Harry Emerson Fosdick, and Brevard Childs.[3] Some, such as Ernst Sellin and Georg Fohrer, asserted that Jonah was no more

3. James D. Smart, "Introduction and Exegesis to the Book of Jonah," in *The Interpreter's Bible*, 12 vols., ed. George Buttrick (New York: Abingdon, 1956), 6:872; R. K. Harrison, *Introduction to the Old Testament* (Grand Rapids: Eerdmans, 1969), p. 918; Harry Emerson Fosdick, *A Guide to Understanding the Bible. The Development of Ideas Within the Old and New Testaments* (New York: Harper & Brothers, 1938), p. 143; and Brevard S. Childs, "Jonah: A Study in Old Testament Hermeneutics," *Scottish Journal of Theology* 11 (1958): 61.

than an expansion of Ezekiel 18:23 to a universal dimension.[4] Ezekiel's message from the Lord was, "Do I take any pleasure in the death of the wicked? Declares the Sovereign LORD. Rather, am I not pleased when they turn from their ways and live?" Sellin and Fohrer thought that Amos's messages and those from the postexilic wisdom movement were influential as well. Thus, they were willing to say that Jonah had an influence on the idea of mission, but that there was no direct teaching on this concept.

Others like Johannes Blauw thought that the missionary concept could be deduced from the Book of Jonah, but what was most evident in the book was Jonah's subtle argument for an anti-particularistic view of God's grace and an anti-nationalistic spirit.[5]

Leslie Allen denied that Jonah was a missionary tract, but curiously he, in the same breath, argued that it provided a firm foundation on which the New Testament mission could build.[6] But how could that be if the book did not originally supply the basis for such a foundation?

A similarly mixed conclusion came from Robert Martin-Achard, who also denied that Jonah illustrated an active mission to the Gentiles, but who nevertheless strangely found a mission for the Christian church. He declared:

> It remains a theological *midrash* whose ultimate meaning will not become apparent until Christ, by living, so to speak, through Jonah's experience in His own death and resurrection, has inaugurated the age of world-evangelization; we shall then be permitted to find a call to the work of mission in this book.[7]

Others have said that Jonah was written to counter the religious exclusivism of Ezra and Nehemiah in the postexilic times.

Moving further out from a mission-minded or universalistic offer of the gospel to the Gentile nations are those scholars who thought that the

4. Ernst Sellin and Georg Fohrer, *Introduction to the Old Testament,* trans. David E. Green (New York: Abingdon, 1968), p. 443. I am beholden to my former student Donald E. Weaver, Jr., *Israel's Mission to the World* (Unpublished Master of Arts Thesis, Trinity Evangelical Divinity School, Deerfield, Ill., 1977).

5. Johannes Blauw, *The Missionary Nature of the Church* (New York: McGraw-Hill, 1962), pp. 34, 41.

6. Leslie C. Allen, *The Books of Joel, Obadiah, Jonah, and Micah* (Grand Rapids: Eerdmans, 1976), p. 193.

7. Robert Martin-Achard, *A Light to the Nations: A Study of the Old Testament Conception of Israel's Mission to the World,* trans. John P. Smith (London: Oliver & Boyd, 1962), pp. 53–54.

emphasis of the Book of Jonah was more on justice as opposed to mercy, or that the theology of divine mercy was conditioned on genuine repentance and a change of heart.[8] Accordingly, the book becomes more about God and man rather than Jew and Gentile.

The Missionary Purpose of the Book of Jonah

It is chapter 4 of the Book of Jonah that answers the question of the purpose of this book. Clearly, the attitude of this reluctant prophet of God is sternly rebuked, for both his narrow provincialism and his stinginess with the grace of God to foreigners. There is also an earlier rebuke to the prophet for failing to obey and to go immediately to Nineveh. The text was written to help others avoid the trap Jonah fell into and to encourage their adoption of Yahweh's heart for the nations—yes, even one's most brutal enemies!

Jonah 4, according to many interpreters, has two paragraphs: verses 1–5 and verses 6–11. Basically, the first paragraph displays Jonah's attitude of intransigence and obstinacy in contrast to the attitude of the Lord. Jonah is violently opposed to any diminishing of the threatened judgment. That is another reason why he did not wish to go to Nineveh in the first place. Should the Ninevites repent and change their hearts, Yahweh would surely withdraw the judgment that Jonah assured them was only forty days away from happening. That would be a tragedy beyond belief. After all, Assyria had inflicted much suffering over the years on Israel. In Jonah's view, this was payback time. So let God do what he said he was going to do. Why warn them and take a chance that even some, much less the whole nation, would repent?

So now, in a real sour-grapes scene, Jonah is pulling an I-told-you-so-posture as chapter 4 opens. He knew that God was "slow to anger and abounding in grace [Hebrew: *ḥesed*], a God who relents from sending calamity." He was hardly the model missionary! Nevertheless, the word of God did triumph despite the prophet's lack of theological application of the universal offer of the gospel or Jonah's penchant for failing to accept the fact that God was also the God of their enemies.

8. In the order supplied above, these conclusions came from Yehezekel Kaufmann, *The Religion of Israel from Its Beginnings to the Babylonian Exile,* trans. Moshe Greenberg (Chicago: University of Chicago Press, 1960), p. 283; Benoit Trepanier, "The Story of Jonas," *Catholic Biblical Quarterly* 13 (1951): 14; and R. E. Clements, "The Purpose of the Book of Jonah," in *Congress Volume, Edinburgh, 1974, Supplements to Vetus Testamentum* 28 (1975): 21.

The second paragraph begins with God's ministry to the prophet. In fact, the final two verses involve both an appeal to Jonah and to each of us as readers. Whose attitude will we adopt: Jonah's or Yahweh's? Jonah expressed concern only for his own comfort and protection, as seen through the episode of the dying plant. But what about all the people, not to mention the cattle and more particularly 120,000 children that still do not know one hand from the other?

Surely this is a missionary appeal. Here is the purpose of the whole book. That purpose is not stated until the very last minute in the story. It is put as a rhetorical question to Jonah, but as a direct one to all who ever read this book. All expostulations against Jonah being a missionary book are vain in light of the force of the questions that come at the end of the book. The question that the prophet and the reader of this book are left with is this: "Should I not be concerned about that great city?" (4:11c).

The Purpose of Jonah's Commission

There can be little doubt that Jonah had functioned already as a witness in Israel when he prophesied to that nation (2 Kings 14:24–25). But why send this messenger to Nineveh when there were such crying needs at home in Israel? Surely their iniquity must have risen to heaven with just as much urgency as that of the Assyrians, if not more. After all, had not the Israelites claimed to know and to walk with this Sovereign Lord? So what was the purpose of sending Jonah, against his will, to such a heathen land when the work in his own land was not yet finished?

The answer lies in the fact that the special work he had to do (against this almost unbounded evil in Assyria) was a sign to Israel of the mind of God. It consisted of a work that was being committed to this ambassador to a people who were clearly outside the territory of Israel, but who likewise needed to be subjected to the call for moral rectitude and godliness.

Of course, there were many other cities that could just as well have been chosen with equal fairness for a similar message. Beside the inscrutable mystery of the sovereignty of God, two special reasons might be listed for choosing Nineveh: (1) the greatness of its population and resources, and (2) the enormity of its crimes. Nineveh was "that great city" whose descriptions both in antiquity and now in modern archaeological terms boggle the mind! A city with some 1,500 towers spaced along the walls rising up to 200 feet high, it contained 120,000 children as well. It was regarded as the height of civilization of that day.

But mark it well: to send a messenger to a city so well-known in its day, with resources that few if any rivaled, was to grab the attention of others besides those to whom the prophet was sent. Whatever would be done here would not be something that was done in a corner. It would be a public example for all the surrounding nations. Few would have ever thought that a city and nation so self-sufficient in itself would ever be capable of being stirred to repentance and reformation. But if this one nation should by any chance respond to the call for repentance, despite the unlikelihood of success, surely that would come as an open rebuke to Israel, who had such superior advantages in the gospel, as well as to the other nations that were just as vulnerable to similar declarations of impending judgment. If the wayward foreigner eagerly received the word from God and acted appropriately, should not the people of God have done at least the same by obeying?

Was this not the very point that our Lord made when he used Nineveh as an example in his preaching? He declared that the people of Nineveh would rise up in the judgment to condemn those who had even greater access to the truth and evidence for the gospel, but who had not also repented as had the people of Nineveh. The task being performed by Jonah was to move his own people to jealousy and action.

This principle, then, is common to all ages. The faith of a Gentile people surpassed that found among the so-called people of God. In that case, the kingdom of God would be taken from the children and given instead to a nation that brought forth the fruits of that kingdom.

This brings us to one of the principles found in missions: mission is one of the means God uses to provoke those who claim to be his people to jealousy and repentance. The image of thousands of heathen casting off their former way of life and crying out to God in repentance is to shame mediocre believers into repentance and mending of their ways. Such is one of our Lord's final and loudest calls to repentance. God is no respecter of persons.

The Mission of Israel to the Nations in Other Prophets

Joel. Joel may be one of the earliest writing prophets, coming somewhere around 835 B.C. in the minority of King Joash. While the date is not all that secure, the word that Joel had about the nations is not unclear. Joel witnessed about a day when God would pour out his Holy Spirit on "all flesh." This expression is so frequently used in a universal fashion in so many contexts that it is hard to limit it to anything less in this setting. To show just how broad that extension was, the prophet announced that this downpour would not be limited by either age, gender, or race. The latter idea is asserted in his reference to "menservants and maidservants." Servants in a Jewish household were not from their own people, but from the Gentiles (2:28–32).

The reference to "all flesh" (Hebrew: *kôl bāśār*) in Joel 2:28 (Hebrew: Joel 3:1) is used in other contexts to indicate a universal scope (e.g., Gen. 6:12, 13, 17; Num. 18:15; Isa. 49:26). Therefore, it is not only the reference to the "menservants" and "maidservants" that broadens the scope of the Spirit of God, but the specific reference to "all flesh." This is also substantiated by the following verse that declares that "everyone who calls" upon the name of the Lord will be saved. The mission of the gospel is as broad as the human race!

Amos. The most significant missiological text in Amos is 9:11–12. There God promised that the fallen "house" of David that had become only a "booth" or "tent" would be repaired and restored "in that day" of God's work in the end times. But this work of restoration would be "so that they may possess the remnant of Edom, even all the nations that bear my name" (v. 12). The Septuagint and one Dead Sea Scroll reading of this text had it that "the remnant of men and the nations that bear my name may seek the LORD." The word for "seek" and "possess" in Hebrew, written in the paleo-script, could easily be confused, for the difference was only in the length of the downward stroke of the letter.[9]

Regardless of which of the two readings is to be preferred (and we usually say the harder reading, which in this case would be the Hebrew "possess"), the possession involved is more than disinheriting one's former enemies. The nations/Gentiles would bear God's very name in either case.

The future of Israel once again would involve a wide nationalism. That is the point that James brought out to end the dispute at the Jerusalem Council (Acts 15:13–18) as he employed this very passage to end the doubts of many about Gentiles being offered the same free grace of God as the Jewish believers were experiencing.

Micah. Micah 4:1–5 contains the famous depiction of all the nations flowing toward the mountain of the Lord. This picture of the effective results of the gospel are in direct juxtaposition to those in Israel who fail

---

9. For a fuller discussion of this text, see Walter C. Kaiser, Jr., "The Davidic Promise and the Inclusion of the Gentiles (Amos 9: 9–15 and Acts 15: 13–18)," *Journal of the Evangelical Theological Society* 20 (1977): 97–111.

in their privilege and responsibilities in the preceding chapters of Micah. The nations will urge, "Come, let us go up to the mountain of the LORD, to the house of the God of Jacob. He will teach us his ways so that we may walk in his paths" (4:2). The effect is awesome: all the nations living by the truth of the Lord God forever and ever!

Isaiah. We have already dealt with the Servant Songs in Isaiah that had such a powerful effect on the theology of missions in the Old Testament. But a quick survey of other chapters bears out the same emphasis. Four allusions are especially noteworthy.[10] First, at the end of Isaiah 11 the picture is one of the whole earth (or world) being full of the knowledge of the Lord. Here is a witness to what Israel's experience was to have as its outcome. The second allusion is even more graphic. In Isaiah 19, as a result of God's healing, Egypt and Assyria will also be a part of God's "blessing" in all the earth. This could well be another allusion to Genesis 12:3. The third reference to Israel's mission is Isaiah 25, which like Micah 4, has Zion as the mountain where "all peoples" (v. 6) come to worship God. Common to all three passages is the fact that God will be exalted among all the nations. Finally, Isaiah 39 is crucial, for Hezekiah failed to give the glory to God before the visiting dignitaries from Babylon. Not only the king, Hezekiah, had failed to give God the glory, but Israel had also failed to be God's witness. The exile that will follow in Babylon would be not only Israel's punishment for her sin, but it would become the vehicle for her to fulfill the mission she had neglected. This idea is central to Isaiah 40–48 and Isaiah 56–66. If Israel was loathe to tell the message of God, they would become visual object lessons so the nations could see for themselves that God was their God, whether in blessing or in a curse.

Jeremiah. The same note is struck in Jeremiah: the nations will gather to Jerusalem to worship the Lord (3:17). The city of Jerusalem "will bring [God] renown, joy, praise, and honor before all nations on earth" (33:9). But if she refused her mission, the nation would sit in exile to fulfill that task of witness that she had so sadly neglected at so many times.

Zechariah. Zechariah 2:11 envisions a coming day when "many nations will be joined to the LORD in that day and will become my people." The same thought is again stated in 8:20–23. The outcome in 14:16–19 will

10. These are suggested by John Oswalt, "The Mission of Israel to the Nations," in *Through No Fault of Their Own? The Fate of Those Who Have Never Heard,* ed. W. V. Crockett and J. G. Sigountos (Grand Rapids: Baker, 1991), pp. 85–95.

have the survivors of the nations, who had been attacking Israel, come with all the people of the earth to worship the Lord in Jerusalem.

Conclusion

Israel was called to be God's witness to the nations. She was to do so by life and demeanor: God's glory was to be seen in his chosen agents of blessing. But they were also to have witnessed these truths in words as well.

The promise of God had been intended for all the nations, indeed, for "all flesh." There were no limitations placed on the scope of that word that was to be issued to all. Only Israel's provincialism and chauvinism forced her into a jaundiced position of envy and partiality. But she was to pay for this by being deliberately scattered among the nations and by being put in exile more than once.

Was Jonah's mission unique then? Hardly. How could God have sent this one prophet abroad and never have thought it worthwhile to send any other prophets? How could the dominant note of Genesis 12:3 be smothered by nationalistic concerns to the detriment of the mission to the world at large? Had not God sent individuals in the past to do exactly this very same thing? Why should his prophets pull punches now?

If Yahweh was the incomparably great God that Isaiah 40–48 declared, how could this be mediated in the nation's mission in any other way than faithfulness to the directive given to that people at the time of their election? It would be through the people of Israel that the nations of the earth were to hear the Good News of the coming Man of Promise and the blessing that God intended for all to hear.

SIX

God's Call to the Missionary Paul Based on the Old Testament

THE APOSTLE Paul stated in the clearest terms possible how he related personally to the older testament. In his trial before Felix (Acts 24:14), he announced, "I believe everything that agrees with the Law and that is written in the Prophets." The apostle never viewed his mission to be something that was brand-new and unattached to what God had been doing in the past or what he wanted to continue to do in the present. The Old Testament was Paul's authoritative source for the mission on which God was sending him. But can this claim be substantiated?

The Legitimation of the Gentile Mission

One of the most prominent themes in the Book of Acts is the mission to the Gentiles. It could be said that this theme is so strong in the book that it appears to be showing how the early believers carried out the command of Jesus in Acts 1:8. It stated: "But you will receive power when the Holy Spirit comes on you; and you will be my witnesses in Jerusalem, and in all Judea and Samaria, and to the ends of the earth." It was this extension to the "ends of the earth" that catches our eye here. What could that imply but a mission to the Gentiles?

Now what is significant about this is the way the writer of Luke and Acts legitimated the Gentile mission by appealing to the older Scriptures. Joseph B. Tyson[1] pointed out six places where such a process of legitimation appeared in the two-volume history of Scripture, Luke–Acts: (1) Jesus' sermon at Nazareth (Luke 4:16–30); (2) the story of the Ethiopian eunuch (Acts 8:26–40); (3) the conclusion to Paul's speech at Pisidian Antioch (Acts 13:44–47); (4) the comments of James at the Jerusalem Council (Acts 15:13–21); (5) Paul's final speech at Rome (Acts 28:23–28); and (6) the conversion of Cornelius (Acts 10:1–11:18). Tyson listed Cornelius last since he felt it was Luke's centerpiece for justifying the Gentile mission in that it did not attempt to reach back into the Old Testament for its justification, as did the other texts.

But we are most interested in Paul and his use of the Old Testament. For example, at Antioch of Pisidia, he announced his decision to turn to the Gentiles (Acts 13:46). But he supported that decision with a quotation from Isaiah 49:6, "I have made you a light to the Gentiles, that you may bring salvation to the ends of the earth" (Acts 13:47). Paul's authority for his action was anchored in the long-term plan of God announced by the eighth-century B.C. prophet.

James, of course, had done the same thing at the Jerusalem Council. Peter's Gentile mission likewise, argued James, was founded on what the eighth-century B.C. prophet Amos had addressed. Amos had intoned:

> In that day I will restore David's fallen tent. I will repair its broken places, restore its ruins, and build it as it used to be, so they may possess the remnant of Edom and all the nations that bear my name, declares the LORD, who will do these things (9:11–12).[2]

Once again the Gentile mission has been affirmed by appealing to the prophetic Scripture.

Paul's final speech at Rome, coming as it does at the conclusion of the Book of Acts, made the same point. As the Jewish leaders came together for the second time to hear Paul, this apostle tried to convince them about

1. Joseph B. Tyson, "The Gentile Mission and the Authority of Scripture in Acts," *New Testament Studies* 33 (1987): 619–31.

2. See Walter C. Kaiser, Jr., "The Davidic Promise and the Inclusion of the Gentiles (Amos 9:1–15 and Acts 15:13–18)," *Journal of the Evangelical Theological Society* 20 (1977): 97–111.

Jesus from the Law of Moses and the prophets. Some were moved by his argument, but not all, by a long shot. To explain this Jewish rejection, Paul appealed to Isaiah 6:9–10. He ended his attempt to convince them with these serious words: "Therefore, I want you to know that God's salvation has been sent to the Gentiles and they will listen!" (Acts 28:28).

On to the Ends of the Earth

Thus far we have established that Paul maintained that his call and ministry to the Gentiles was anchored in the Old Testament. All the promises of God found in the Old Testament have their "Yes" in Jesus Christ (2 Cor. 1:20). In fact, Jesus was the One to which the Law pointed (Rom. 10:4) and the gospel Paul preached was the same which God had "promised beforehand through his prophets in the holy Scriptures" (Rom. 1:1–2). This gospel was the instrument through which the Gentiles from "among all the nations" would come to believe in Jesus as the Messiah (Rom. 1:5).

In a most interesting article, Roger D. Aus[3] explored the Old Testament exegetical background that lay behind the apostle's thinking about the "full number of the Gentiles" in Romans 11:25. Paul declared that "a hardening had come over part of Israel until the full number of the Gentiles had come in." Only after this event would "all Israel be saved" (Rom. 11:26). Aus argued that that number was arrived at when Paul went to Spain, thereby going to what was equated at the time with going to "the ends of the earth." Aus also tied in the concept of the "offering of the Gentiles" of Romans 15:16 with this concept as well, but not all of Aus's ideas appear to bear the full weight of the text.

There is no question that the apostle did aspire to reach Spain, for he explicitly stated the same in Romans 15:24, 28. As he wrote the epistle to the Romans from Greece, he stated that he would "pass through" (Greek: *diaporeuomenos*) the capital of the Roman Empire, but his real goal was Spain.

As Paul traveled along his journey, he gathered, from the various Christian churches he had founded, Gentiles whose priestly services for the gospel of God he regarded as "fruit" (Rom. 15:16). These converts Paul saw as an "offering of the Gentiles" and a proof of his service (Rom. 15:31).

3. Roger D. Aus, "Paul's Travel Plans to Spain and the 'Full Number of the Gentiles' of Rom. XI 25," *Novum Testamentum* 21 (1979): 232–62.

In Aus's view, the Gentiles of the end times were to bring Jews from nations wherever the diaspora was found, but Paul would bring Gentile Christians, not Jews, to Jerusalem as an offering to the Lord Jesus. Paul obtained this idea from Isaiah 66:21, Aus declared.

Spain was regarded as the "end(s) of the earth." For example, when Jonah boarded a ship for Tarshish or Spain, he thought it was at that point that he would be far away from the presence of the Lord (Jonah 1:3). The same connection between Tarshish/Spain and the ends of the earth is seen in Psalm 72:8–11. It observed:

> He will rule from sea to sea
> and from the River to the ends of the earth.
> The desert tribes will bow down before him
> and his enemies will lick the dust.
> The kings of Tarshish and of distant shores
> will bring tribute to him;
> the kings of Sheba and Seba will present him gifts.
> All kings will bow down to him
> and all nations will serve him.

The "River" here is the Euphrates or what many regarded in Israel as the far east, while the kings of Tarshish were thought to be the farthest point west, indeed, at "the ends of the earth." To pass through the Straits of Gibraltar between Spain and Africa (known as the Pillars of Hercules) was to pass into the end of the earth, according to many ancients.

Isaiah 66:18

Tarshish, or Spain as it is known today, appears again in Isaiah 66:18. The nations of the west, presumably in the "ships of Tarshish" (1 Kings 10:22; Isa. 60:9), will bring not only the sons of Israel back to their homeland once again; they will also carry the Gentiles with their wealth, their gold, and their frankincense as offerings to the Lord (Isa. 60:3–9).

Of course, the complete realization of this forecast will come in that eschatological day. But Matthew's account of the wise men who came from the east with gold, frankincense, and myrrh for the one who was born "king of the Jews" (Matt. 2:1–12) is but a foretaste of what was to come. As Aus notes, this bringing of gifts from distant lands for "King" Messiah was known much before the birth of Christ.

Had not Isaiah 60:5 indicated that the "wealth of the sea"[4] and the "riches of the nations will come" to Jerusalem? Thus, the kings, representing the people, led the procession to Jerusalem with their wealth in hand as an offering to Yahweh.

The distinctive contribution of Aus is his unique connection of the phrase "the full number of the Gentiles" in Romans 11:25 with the phrase in Isaiah 60:5, "the wealth of the seas/west/sunset/evening." The reason for Aus's connecting these texts is twofold. (1) In Romans 11:25, Paul quotes in the very next verse Isaiah 59:20–21. That text read:

> "The Redeemer will come to Zion,
> to those in Jacob who will repent of their sins,"
> declares the LORD.
> As for me, this is my covenant with them, says the LORD:
> "My Spirit, who is on you,
> and my words that I put in your mouth
> will not depart from your mouth,
> or from the mouths of your children,
> or from the mouths of their descendants
> from this time on and forever," says the LORD.

Paul quoted this passage in Romans 11:26, saying,

> And so all Israel will be saved,
> as it is written:
> "The Deliverer will come from Zion;
> he will turn godlessness away from Jacob.
> And this is my covenant with them
> when I take away their sins."

Note that Jesus is that "Redeemer" who is here called a "Deliverer," who comes not "to" Zion, but "from" it.

(2) Only five verses after this quotation from Isaiah 59:20–21 is the citation from Isaiah 60:5, which Aus believes influenced the reading in Romans 11:25 about the "full number of the Gentiles." In Isaiah 60:5, the word for "wealth" is a singular noun that has a plural verb linked with it in a most unusual Hebrew combination. Even more fascinating, Aus

---

4. Aus, "Paul's Travel Plans," p. 250, notes that the Targum of Isaiah on this verse read "the wealth of the *west*." This would agree with verse 9, where the ships of Tarshish came from the west as well.

pointed out that one Greek translation of the Hebrew text, Sinaiticus, read instead of "wealth," a "large number" (Greek: *plēthos*), which would only be a small step for the apostle Paul to derive "full number" (Greek: *plērōma*) from it. The Greek word for "wealth" is *ploutos*. Aus's point is that the "wealth" that is being brought to Jerusalem is nothing less than the Gentiles themselves—and that in "full number," or as Sinaiticus has it, in a "large number."

If this most interesting exegesis is correct, then Paul's mission to the Gentiles was a direct effort to prepare this huge offering as a veritable sacrifice offered to the Living God. Clearly it was Paul's practice to gather together delegates from each area he went to evangelize so they could bring the offerings he had collected as gifts to Jerusalem. They only typified the harvest of Gentiles that were being won to the Lord. Aus wanted to connect this practice with Psalm 68:29, Isaiah 60:11, and Jeremiah 3:14. But that connection seems less probable, even if it is ingenious.

Aus has one final step in his most interesting argument. "The full number of Gentiles" for Paul will come only after he has gone to "the ends of the earth," which was understood in many contexts of that day to be Spain. After he had ministered in Spain, Aus assured us, then the Messiah would come, according to Paul's thinking.[5] Not only would the missionary movement be over, but so would the present age come to an end as well.

But this, too, is a stretch. It argues that Paul thought the Messiah would surely come during his lifetime and only later did he begin to lose hope in this thesis. This is not the place for a full refutation of that idea, for our task is to get at Paul's use of the Old Testament for authorizing his Gentile mission.

Romans 15:8–12

A stronger case can be made from Paul's direct statement in Romans 15:8–12. There Paul took pains to ground his message and mission in the Old Testament. For him, this was the climax to the soteriological (i.e. salvation) tract, the Book of Romans. He declared:

> For I tell you that Christ has become a servant of the Jews
> on behalf of God's truth, to confirm the promises made to
> the patriarchs [Abraham, Isaac, and Jacob] so that the
> Gentiles may glorify God for his mercy, as it is written:

5. Aus, "Paul's Travel Plans," pp. 260–61.

"Therefore I will praise you among the Gentiles;
I will sing hymns to your name." (2 Sam. 22:50; Ps. 18:49)

Again it says,

"Rejoice, O Gentiles, with his people." (Deut. 32:43)

And again,

"Praise the Lord, all you Gentiles,
and sing praises to him, all you peoples." (Ps. 117:1)

And again, Isaiah says,

"The Root of Jesse will spring up,
one who will arise to rule over the nations;
the Gentiles will hope in him." (Isa. 11:10)

Paul is arguing here, " Don't you understand what is happening in our work and our mission? Christ has become a servant of his people Israel, the Jews; and this is on behalf of confirming the truth God gave to the patriarchs. It is that in his promised seed, all the families of the earth might be blessed as he promised in Genesis 12:3. God's philosophy of history is that the Gentiles also may come to glorify God for his mercy. The five Old Testament texts that he strings together (2 Sam. 22:50; Ps. 18:49; Deut. 32:43; Ps. 117:1; Isa. 11:10) all are shouting, "Don't you get the point about the Gentiles/nations? This is at the heart of my plan of salvation for the world."

The Gentile mission was not some sort of *ab extra,* an add-on; it had always been at the heart of all that God had wanted to do and had called Israel and all believers to do. This was why God was working through his Son. It was on behalf of the truth, which truth was to confirm his promise made to the ancient fathers of the nation of Israel, Abraham, Isaac, and Jacob.

Conclusion

Paul was the missionary to the Gentiles par excellence. The same gospel that had been given by the prophets in the Holy Scriptures was now the Good News that Paul carried to the nations.

In the plan of God, there was a "full number of the Gentiles" that must first come to know the Savior. But this coming was to cause the Jewish people to become jealous. However, when that number had been reached, then God would once again turn to the Jewish people (Rom. 11:11–12, 25–26).

But there could be no mistaking where Paul got his marching orders: they came from the Old Testament. The case for evangelizing the Gentiles had not been a recently devised switch in the plan of God, but had always been the long-term commitment of the Living God who is a missionary God. This is the same case that is consistently, even if at times only rudimentarily, found in the entire corpus of the Old Testament.

Glossary

Accommodation—The term preferred by Roman Catholic missiologists (rather than indigenous) entailing the adapting or adjusting a culture to fit a particular church tradition.

Carey, William—(1761–1834) The father of the modern missionary movement who wrote in 1792 the famous treatise, *An Inquiry into the Obligation of Christians to Use Means For the Conversion of the Heathens,* which became the marching orders for modern missions.

Centrifugal—"Outward-moving." This is the word used to describe the active work of Old Testament believers to aggressively take the message of the Good News about the coming Man of Promise to the Gentile world around them.

Centripetal—"Inward-moving." A term used to describe the more passive attitude many think they observe in the Old Testament obligation to witness to the Gentiles. Instead, the burden rested on the unreached to take the initiative to become converts to the faith according to this view.

Church—A body of believers who have voluntarily joined together for the purpose of glorifying the Name of God and for spreading the Good News of the gospel to humanity.

Contextualization—A term describing how the gospel message engages the culture, particularly as it relates to social issues. It is that program by which missionaries should communicate the gospel and plant churches untainted (as much as possible) by the missionary's own culture.

Covenant—A compact or agreement made between individuals that may be either one-sided (unilateral), with all responsibility for maintaining it left with the promising party, God, or two-sided (bilateral), with responsibility for its maintenance resting on both contracting parties.

Great Commission—The mandate left by our Lord in five versions of this Commission to finish the task of going into all the world and teaching the Good News of Christ's gospel. The five places where this Commission is repeated are Matthew 28:19–20; Mark 16:15; Luke 24:46–49; John 20:21; and Acts 1:8.

Indigeneity (or indigenous)—An agricultural term that describes how a plant thrives in a particular culture or climate, but when applied to missions metaphorically it relates to how churches are able to thrive within their own cultures when planted by missionaries.

Kingdom of God—The state and sphere of the rule and reign of God that has begun already and will embrace everything in that final day. The church is called to be a missionary agent of God's kingdom in this world.

Mission—The set of beliefs, theories, and aims of a particular sending body of the Christian world that determines the character, purpose, organization, strategy, and action to evangelize the unreached world for Christ and to minister holistically to its needs.

Missionary Call—A summons from God to share Christ with the unreached peoples of the earth (Eph. 4:4–11).

Missiology—The academic discipline that treats the history, theory, strategy, and expansion of Christianity among non-Christians from the standpoint of a biblical theology.

Septuagint—Also called the "Seventy" and abbreviated LXX. It is the Greek translation of the Hebrew Bible made in Alexandria, Egypt, sometime during the third to first centuries B.C.

Patriarch—Term for the male head of a family in the ancient Near East; originally applied to the three "fathers" of Israel: Abraham, Isaac, and Jacob.

Pentateuch—This term, meaning "five scrolls," is the Greek word for the first five books of the Hebrew Bible: Genesis, Exodus, Leviticus, Numbers, and Deuteronomy.

Polytheism—The belief that there are many gods and not just One.

Sanhedrin—The final judicial body of the Jews from the third century B.C. until the Romans destroyed Jerusalem in A.D. 70.

Synagogue—The gathering place for Jews in instruction or worship that arose during the Babylonian exile and continued into modern times.

Targum—The Aramaic paraphrase of the Hebrew Bible completed sometime early in the Christian era.

Torah—Hebrew term meaning "instruction," "teaching," or "law." It may be used in a general sense of all the canonical writings of the Old Testament or especially of the first five books of the Hebrew Bible.

Zion—The name for the "citadel" or rocky ridge in old Jerusalem that later became the poetical way of referring to the city of Jerusalem itself.

Bibliography

Aalders, G. Ch. *The Problem of the Book of Jonah*. London: Tyndale House, 1948.

Adrian, V. "The Missionary Message of the Old Testament." In *The Church in Mission: A Sixtieth Anniversary Tribute to J. S. Toews*. Ed. A. J. Klassen. Fresno, Calif., 1967, pp. 17–32.

Allis, Oswald T. "The Blessing of Abraham." *Princeton Theological Review* 25 (1927): 263–98.

Arias, Mortimar. "Centripetal Mission or Evangelism by Hospitality." *Missiology: An International Review* 10 (1982): 69–81.

Aus, Roger D. "Paul's Travel Plans to Spain and the 'Full Number of the Gentiles' of Rom. XI 25." *Novum Testamentum* 21 (1979): 232–62.

Baldwin, Joyce. "Malachi 1:11 and the Worship of the Nations in the Old Testament." *Tyndale Bulletin* 23 (1972): 117–24.

Bertram, G. "Ethnos." In *Theological Dictionary of the New Testament*. Ed. G. Kittel. 10 vols. Grand Rapids: Eerdmans, 1964, 2:364–69.

Beuken, W. A. M. "*Mishpat:* The Servant Song in Its Context." *Vetus Testamentum* 22 (1972): 6ff.

Blauw, Johannes. *The Missionary Nature of the Church*. New York: McGraw-Hill, 1962.

Bower, William Paul. "Studies in Paul's Understanding of His Mission." Ph.D. dissertation, University of Cambridge, Cambridge, England, 1976.

Braude, W. G. *Jewish Proselytizing in the First Five Centuries of the Common Era*. Providence, R.I.: Brown University Press, 1940.

Childs, Brevard S. "Jonah: A Study in Old Testament Hermeneutics." *Scottish Journal of Theology* 11 (1958): 53–61.

Clements, R. E. "Goi." In *Theological Dictionary of the Old Testament*. Ed. G. Johannes Botterweck and Helmer Ringgren. 8 vols. Grand Rapids: Eerdmans, 1975, 2:426–33.

_____. "The Purpose of the Book of Jonah." *Supplements to Vetus Testamentum* 28 (1975): 16–28.

DeRidder, Richard R. *Discipling the Nations*. Grand Rapids: Baker, 1976.

Dobbie, R. "Biblical Foundations of the Mission of the Church: I: The Old Testament." *International Review of Missions* 51 (1962): 196–205.

DuBose, Francis M. *God Who Sends: A Fresh Quest for Biblical Mission*. Nashville, Tenn.: Broadman, 1983.

Ellington, John. "Send!" *The Bible Translator* 45 (1994): 228–38.

Ellison, H. L. "Is the Book of Jonah a Missionary Pamphlet?" *Bulletin of Evangelical Fellowship for Missionary Studies* 1 (1972): 31–36.

Fairbairn, Patrick. *Jonah: His Life, Character and Mission*. Edinburgh: John Johnstone, 1849.

Filbeck, David. *Yes, God of the Gentiles, Too: The Missionary Message of the Old Testament*. Wheaton, Ill.: Billy Graham Center, Wheaton College, 1994.

Fraine, J. de. "Les nations paiennes dans les Psaumes." *Studi sull' Oriente e la Biblia, offerti al P. Giovanni Rinaldi*. Genoa, 1967, pp. 285–92.

Gelston, A. "The Missionary Message of Second Isaiah." *Scottish Journal of Theology* 18 (1965): 308–18.

Gervaryahu, H. "The Universalism of the Book of Jonah." *Dor le Dor* 10 (1981): 20–27.

Greenberg, Moshe. "Mankind, Israel and the Nations in Hebraic Heritage." In *No Man is Alien*. Ed. J. Robert Nelson. Leiden: Brill, 1971, pp. 15–40.

Grisanti, Michael A. "Israel's Mission to the Nations in Isaiah 40–55: An Update." *The Master's Seminary Journal* 9 (1998): 39–61.

Halas, Roman. "The Universalism of Isaias." *Catholic Biblical Quarterly* 12 (1950): 162–70.

Hamlin, E. J. "Nations in Second Isaiah." *Southeastern Journal of Theology* 2 (1960): 37–48.

Hempel, J. "Die Wurzeln des Missionswillens im Glauben des Alten Testaments." *Zeitschrift für Alten Testamentum* 66 (1954): 244–72.

Hollenberg, D. E. "Nationalism and 'The Nations' in Isaiah XL–LV." *Vetus Testamentum* 19 (1969): 23–36.

Jeremias, Joachim. *Jesus' Promise to the Nations*. London: SCM, 1958.

_____. "Pais Theou in Later Judaism in the Period after the LXX." In *Theological Dictionary of the New Testament*. Ed. G. Kittle. Grand Rapids: Eerdmans, 1967, 5:677–700.

Johnson, Dennis E. "Jesus Against the Idols: The Use of Isaianic Servant Songs in the Missiology of Acts." *Westminster Theological Journal* 52 (1990): 343–53.

Kaiser, Walter C., Jr. "Israel's Missionary Call." In *Perspectives on the World Christian Mission*. Ed. Ralph D. Winter and Steven C. Hawthorne. Pasadena, Calif.: William Carey Library, 1981, pp. 25–34.

———. *Toward an Old Testament Theology*. Grand Rapids: Zondervan, 1978.

———. "The Davidic Promise and the Inclusion of the Gentiles (Amos 9:9–15 and Acts 15:13–18)." *Journal of the Evangelical Theological Society* 20 (1977): 97–111.

———. "The Blessing of David: A Charter for Humanity." In *The Law and the Prophets*. Ed. John Skilton. Philadelphia: Presbyterian & Reformed, 1974, pp. 298–318.

———. "The Old Testament as the Plan of Salvation." In *Toward Rediscovering the Old Testament*. Grand Rapids: Zondervan, 1987, pp. 121–44.

———. "Salvation in the Old Testament: With Special Emphasis on the Object and Content of Personal Belief." *Jian Dao: A Journal of Bible and Theology* 2 (1994): 1–18.

———. "Balaam, Son of Beor, in Light of Deir 'Alla and Scripture: Saint or Soothsayer?" In *Go to the Land I Will Show You: Dwight Young Festschrift*. Ed. Joseph Coleson and Victor Matthews. Winona Lake, Ind.: Eisenbrauns, 1996, pp. 95–106.

Kidner, Derek. " 'A Light to the Nations': Israel and the Gentiles as an Old Testament Theme." *Bulletin of Evangelical Fellowship for Missionary Studies* 1 (1972): 15–21.

Kuhn, Karl Georg. "Proselytos." In *Theological Dictionary of the New Testament*. Ed. G. Kittel. Grand Rapids: Eerdmans, 1968, 6:727–44.

Lamarche, P. *The Salvation of the Gentiles and the Prophets*. Montreal: Palm, 1966.

Lapham, Henry A. *The Bible as Missionary Handbook*. Cambridge: W. Heffer & Sons, 1925.

Lewis, Art H. "Jehovah's International Love." *Journal of the Evangelical Theological Society* 15 (1972): 87–92.

Lind, Millard C. "Refocusing Theological Education to Mission: The Old Testament and Contextualization." *Missiology* 10 (1982): 141–60.

McDaniel, Ferris L. "Mission in the Old Testament." In *Mission in the New Testament: An Evangelical Approach*. Ed. William J. Larkin, Jr., and Joel F. Williams. Maryknoll, N.Y.: Orbis, 1998, pp. 11–29.

McKnight, Scot. *A Light Among the Gentiles: Jewish Missionary Activity in the Second Temple Period*. Minneapolis, Minn.: Fortress, 1990.

Maier, Walter A., III. "The Healing of Naaman in Missiological Perspective." *Concordia Theological Quarterly* 61 (1997): 177–96.

Manson, William. "The Biblical Doctrine of Mission." *International Review of Missions* 42 (1953): 257–65.

Manson, T. W. *Only to the House of Israel? Jesus and the Non-Jews.* Philadelphia: Fortress, 1964.

Marlowe, W. Creighton. "The Music of Missions: Themes of Cross-Cultural Outreach in the Psalms." *Missiology* 26 (1998): 445–56.

Martin-Achard, Robert. "Israel's Mission to the Nations." *International Review of Missions* 51 (1962): 482–84.

_____. *A Light to the Nations: A Study of the Old Testament Conception of Israel's Mission to the World.* Trans. John P. Smith. London: Oliver & Boyd, 1962.

May, Herbert G. "Theological Universalism in the Old Testament." *Journal of Bible and Religion* 16 (1948): 100–107.

May, P. "Towards a Biblical Theology of Missions." *The Indian Journal of Theology* 8 (1959): 21–28.

Morgenstern, Julian, "Universalism and Particularism." In *The Universal Jewish Encyclopedia.* New York: Universal Jewish Encyclopedia Co., 1939–43, 10:353–57.

Moye, J. E. L. "Israel and the Nations in Isaiah 40–77." Th.D. dissertation, Southern Baptist Theological Seminary, 1972.

Muilenberg, James. "Abraham and the Nations: Blessing and World History." *Interpretation* 19 (1965): 387–98.

North, R. "Centrifugal and Centripetal Tendencies in the Judaic Cradle of Christianity." In *Populus Dei, Studi in Onore del Card. Alfredo Ottaviani: I: Israel.* Rome, 1969, pp. 615–51.

Odendaal, D. H. "The Eschatological Expectation of Isaiah 40–66 with Special Reference to Israel and the Nations." Th.D. dissertation, Westminster Theological Seminary, Philadelphia, 1966.

Orlinsky, Harry M. "'A Light to the Nations': A Problem in Biblical Theology." *The Seventy-Fifth Anniversary Volume of the Jewish Quarterly Review.* Ed. A. A. Neuman and S. Zeitlin. Philadelphia, 1967, pp. 409–28.

_____. "Nationalism—Universalism and Internationalism in Ancient Israel." In *Translating and Understanding the Old Testament. Essays in Honor of Herbert Gordon May.* Ed. H. T. Frank and W. L. Reed. Nashville: Abingdon, 1970, pp. 206–36. Also in *Essays in Biblical Culture and Bible Translation.* New York: Ktav, 1974, pp. 133ff.

_____. "Nationalism—Universalism in the Book of Jeremiah." In *Understanding the Sacred Text. Essays in Honor of Morton S. Enslin.* Ed. J. Reumann. Valley Forge, Pa., 1972, pp. 61–83.

Oswalt, John. "The Mission of Israel to the Nations." In *Through No Fault of Their Own? The Fate of Those Who Have Never Heard.* Ed. W. V. Crockett and J. G. Sigountos. Grand Rapids: Baker, 1991, pp. 85–95.

Peck, J. R. "The Missionary View of the Old Testament." *Theological Students' Fellowship Bulletin* 54 (1969): 4–8.

Peters, George. *A Biblical Theology of Missions.* Chicago: Moody, 1972.

Piper, John. *Let the Nations Be Glad! The Supremacy of God in Missions.* Grand Rapids: Baker, 1993.

Preuss, Horst, *"'elilim."* In *Theological Dictionary of the Old Testament.* Ed. G. Johannes Botterweck and Helmer Ringgren, trans. John T. Willis. Grand Rapids: Eerdmans, 1974, 1:285–87.

Rowley, H. H. *Israel's Mission to the World.* London: Student Christian Movement Press, 1939.

———. *The Missionary Message of the Old Testament.* London: Carey Kingsgate, 1944.

Scobbie, Charles H. H. "Israel and the Nations: An Essay in Biblical Theology." *Tyndale Bulletin* 43 (1992): 283–305.

Senior, D., and C. Stuhlmueller. *The Biblical Foundations for Mission.* Grand Rapids: Eerdmans, 1983.

Shank, David. "Jesus the Messiah: Messianic Foundation of Mission." In *The Transfiguration of Mission: Biblical, Theological and Historical Foundations.* Ed. Wilbert R. Shenk. Scottdale, Pa.: Herald, 1993, pp. 37–82.

Shusterman, Abraham. "Mission of Israel." In *The Universal Jewish Encyclopedia.* New York: Universal Jewish Encyclopedia Co., 1939–43, 7:582–84.

Stek, John. "The Message of the Book of Jonah." *Calvin Theological Journal* 4 (1969): 23–50.

Stroud, B. L. "Yahweh and the Nations: A Study of the Relationship of Yahweh to the Non-Israelite." Ph.D. dissertation, Hebrew Union College, 1970.

Terry, John Mark. "Old Testament Foundations for Missions." In *Missiology: An Introduction to the Foundations, History, and Strategies of World Missions.* Ed. John Mark Terry, Ebbie Smith, and Justice Anderson. Nashville, Tenn.: Broadman & Holman, 1998, pp. 51–62.

Thompson, J. W. "The Gentile Mission as an Eschatological Necessity." *Restoration Quarterly* 14 (1971): 18–27.

Tyson, Joseph B. "The Gentile Mission and the Authority of Scripture in Acts." *New Testament Studies* 33 (1987): 619–31.

Van Ruler, A. A. *The Christian Church and the Old Testament.* Grand Rapids: Eerdmans, 1971.

Verkuyl, J. *Contemporary Missiology.* Grand Rapids: Eerdmans, 1978.

Vogels, Walter. "Covenant and Universalism: Guide for a Missionary Reading of the Old Testament." *Zeitschrift für Missionswissenschaft und Religionswissenschaft* 57 (1973): 25–32.

_____. *God's Universal Covenant: A Biblical Study.* Ottawa: University of Ottawa, 1979.

Widbin, R. Bryan. "Salvation for People Outside Israel's Covenant?" In *Through No Fault of Their Own? The Fate of Those Who Have Never Heard.* Ed. W. V. Crockett and J. G. Sigountos. Grand Rapids: Baker, 1991, pp. 73–83.

Wilson, Robert Dick. "The Authenticity of Jonah." *Princeton Theological Review* 16 (1918): 645–54.

Winkle, Dwight Wayne Van. "The Relationship of the Nations to Yahweh and to Israel in Isaiah XL–LV." *Vetus Testamentum* 35 (1985): 446–58.

Wodecki, Bernard. "ŠHLH. dans lle livre d'Isaie." *Vetus Testamentum* 34 (1984): 482–88.

_____. "Heilsuniversalismus im Buch des Propheten Jesaja." In *Dein Wort Bedachten: Alttestamentliche Aufsatze.* Ed. J. Reindl and G. Henschel. Leipzig: St. Benno-Verlag, 1981, pp. 76–101.

Wright, G. Ernest. "The Old Testament Basis for the Christian Mission." In *The Theology of the Christian Mission.* Ed. G. H. Anderson. New York: McGraw-Hill, 1961, pp. 17–30.

Scripture Index

Subject Index

Author Index

101

Walter C. Kaiser, Jr. is president and Colman M. Mockler Distinguished Professor of Old Testament at Gordon-Conwell Theological Seminary. He is the author or coauthor of numerous books, including *Toward an Exegetical Theology* and *A History of Israel.*